Helen Braid was born in Liverpool and has made her home in Scotland. She has degrees in English and Drama, and Educational Psychology and is the author of several non-fiction books and journals. She is currently a researcher, freelance journalist, and writer, and her interests include music and gardening.

Letters to My
Semi-Detached Son
Helen Braid

First published by The Women's Press Ltd, 1993
A member of the Namara Group
34 Great Sutton Street, London EC1V ODX

British Library Cataloguing-in-Publication Data
A catalogue record for this book is available
from the British Library

ISBN 0 7043 4339 8

Typeset in 13/14pt Perpetua Roman by
The Electronic Book Factory Ltd, Fife, Scotland
Printed and bound in Great Britain by
Cox & Wyman Ltd, Reading, Berks.

. . . The crisis
Of the sorrow of so many years is all that
tires me.

Emily Dickinson

You threw me out when I was fifteen years old because of a few lies and an all-night party. Since Jim came, you've never wanted me.
(*Tom's version*)

You threw yourself out because you refused to change. You resisted us to the bitter end. You had to find out if the grass on the other side was really greener.
(*My version*)

Prologue

Dear Tom,

The flat is filled with your absence. The emptiness is tangible. Today you will not come home, sullen and silent in your man-size ten boots to stamp on our house rules, our principles, our way of living. You will not glare at me, or snarl at me, or slam the door on me. You will not mock my appearance, my work, my friends. You will not swear at me, or drown me in your waves of hostility. You will not lie to me. You will not be here at all. I grieve for you. And for myself because I have failed as a mother.

Only days ago you were here, picking up your cardboard boxes of clothes and posters and tapes. Pacing down the cold concrete stairs of the tenement. Down again and again, carrying your belongings. Carrying away your present and your past in the straggling dusty piles you had thrown together. There was no sorting. No buying of suitcases. No consultation over what to keep and what to discard. No helping hand with the packing. Just a furious tumble of things hurled with their memories into black hefty bags. By that stage we were beyond speaking to each other.

The Headband journeyed up in anger and disbelief to

collect you. Finally it sunk in that I meant what I said, that it was him or the streets. I presume he helped you, a hand on your slim shoulders, that he muttered consoling words. But really he is white-mad to have this decision thrust upon him. I imagine him beside you, bearded jaw clamped shut, scurrying in sandals and affected helpfulness. He has not had to be a father for so many years.

As I stand in the new silence of your room, I see a boy of fifteen with long fair hair obliterating vision, perhaps hiding tears, stomping up and down the tenement steps. A boy trying to shrug off the reality of what is happening to him. A boy in unlaced Doc Martens and a grubby black T-shirt, leaving behind an uneasy childhood and a stormy adolescence.

Today I leant against the closed door of your room and released the oceans of tears I have held in for days. I wept for the first uncomplicated years. I wept for the troubled years, after I left The Headband, taking you with me. I wept for your going.

Part 1: Childhood

Dear Tom,

The night before you were born The Headband and I went to the Filmhouse. I remember I wore a long Indian dress printed with deep red and blue flowers over my vast belly. You had grown incredibly heavy. I felt your live, moving form inside me. We were joyful. We awaited your arrival with longing.

Little one, you were very much wanted.

You were my first born and I loved you dearly. A Christmas Eve child, celebrated with sherry in medicine glasses, mistletoe over my bed. It was one of the happiest weeks I have ever spent. You, the son I had secretly ordered. You, healthy and safe beside me in your little plastic fish-tank. You, the most beautiful one of them all. Other babies were blue and purple and wrinkled with little-old-man faces. You had smooth skin and blue eyes and a fuzz of white-fair hair. For three years after your birth I couldn't watch the birth of a child on TV or on film without bursting into tears.

It was one of those bright, frosty Decembers. Each morning as the sun flooded from a clear blue sky on to my counterpane, I picked you up and walked with you to the window. Holding you close, breathing in the sweet milky smell of you, I stood gazing and smiling out of the window. I felt confident. I felt elated. Each day was punctuated with small simple rituals, like collecting the laundry – fresh, warm-ironed nighties with the strings to tie across your tiny back. Or folding you, tight and swaddled, inside a square of white linen, until only your round head stuck out, like a peg-doll or a lollipop. Or putting you down to sleep on your side, or picking you up to feed. In the evenings The Headband brought flowers and bumptiousness, champagne and pride. He rested his feet on the window-sill and propped you upright on his knees so he could pull faces at you. He didn't hold his child gingerly like other new dads. He got right down to the business of making contact with you. His input had already begun.

For the first few years of your life you lived a standard story-book existence. There was Mummy Bear and Daddy Bear and Baby Bear and they lived in a pretty little cottage with pink roses round the door. Our house was last but one in a row of terraces with adjoining narrow back gardens which sloped down to a tranquil pool of water. Around the pool the houses lay in a deep bowl of land, sheltered and invisible from the surrounding network of roads. Your life had a rhythm which kept gentle pace with the seasons. In spring you watched the moorhens build their nests and hatch their young on the small island of willow trees or, more dangerously, amongst the reeds at the edge of the water. In summer you watched the birds teach their chicks to hop across the lily-pads on legs like thin black lines while the dull click of wood echoed from the bowling green close by. In autumn you watched the old men rake up the leaves and play their last games in the setting sun. You counted the chicks which had survived to September. And all year round you ran down the garden and on to that circular path around the pool to meet your father carrying his briefcase home from work.

I thought you were happy then. Like other small children you had your own special friend who seemed to prefer our home to his. One day, curious, he came to visit from further along the street, and then just kept coming. Do you remember his unique method of arrival? He used to tear up and down the pavement outside our house a few times, head down, short stout legs in red sandals pedalling furiously. Then lots of noisy skidding and the bike hauled round on its front wheel, and a slower pedalling back and forth near our fence. Finally eyes right and a forthright stare down into our windows to see if you were there.

'Is Tom there?'

Yes.

'Is Tom playing?'

Yes.

You two small maniacs bumped your bikes down the steep front steps until my heart was in my mouth. Or, worse, you conducted Le Mans races on plastic tractors and trikes down the path towards the pool, races which inevitably ended with him intact but you in tears on the wrong side of the privet hedge.

'Please be careful!' I wailed, as other mums have done. 'Please don't go so fast.'

And, like other kids, neither of you took the slightest notice.

Sometimes the two of you played 'Bear! Bear!' You

would creep up the stairs, hands cupped to giggling mouths, then hide under the bedclothes in the double bed. You hid there until your bodies were hot and sticky and your hearts were beating wildly. You clung together, waiting until the moment was right. Then, with a theatrical gasp and heart-stopping scream, Peter would sit bolt upright: 'Bear! Bear!' he would howl. He would stare wide-eyed, rigid, at the dreadful animal conjured up at the bottom of the bed. For you, little one, it was all too real. Your eyes grew over-bright and red blobs burned on your cheeks. At night in bed you trembled. You said the red-mouthed fox would creep from the pool and climb the creeper at your window. You believed it would hide its whine in the wind. It would open its jaws and eat you while you slept.

Through those first years you had no fears more dreadful than the red-mouthed fox, and no reason to weep except about grazed knees.

Dear Tom,

You are three years old. The houses on the opposite side of the pool have disappeared behind a criss-cross of leaves as if a child like you took a thick green crayon and scribbled a bit more each day over the winter drawing beneath. The geese are giving their young flying lessons, dangerously, weaving in and out of the telegraph wires. The sides of the pool have sprouted faded umbrellas overnight, like oversized mushrooms. The fishing season has begun.

You watch the birds on the water from your bedroom

window. After breakfast I hold your hand and take you down to the railings so that you can feed them your crusts. I hold you up and feel the silk of your straight hair brushing my face. Usually The Headband leaves much earlier for work, but today he lingers with us at our feeding post. He throws crusts way out to the moorhens waiting nervously to scavenge for their young. Your bits of bread land only a few inches away to be snatched by greedy sparrows amongst the reeds. But you are satisfied.

That particular morning we notice a cluster of people standing close to the hedge further round the pool. Someone says, 'One of them ducklings is injured.' We look where they are pointing and see a yellow chick floating oddly in the water. Its neck is twisted sideways, its head hanging back, pulling in its wake a thin dark trail across the pool. Nobody does anything. The chick's head begins to go under. It struggles, hopelessly, to hold it clear of the water.

Someone says, 'I expect a fox got it in the night.'

The duckling battles, still, to lift its lolling head on a floppy useless neck but it drifts further out from the edge of the pool. It looks beaten. So what does your father do? With one scornful, sneering gaze he dismisses the passive group of onlookers and turns on his heel. He stomps off, thick black strands of hair falling over his face, using his arms to propel himself along, a bit like a manic windmill. We knew when he walked like that it was because he was angry, or late, or the arthritis in his feet was bad.

Tied up at the edge of the pool is an old tub of a boat which the fishermen use once a year for clearing out the slimy, choking pondweed. You trot along beside your father and help push the boat out into the water. You watch him jump clumsily in, soaking sandals and jeans, then row with furious energy to the struggling bird. You watch him lift it out of the pool, gently, cradling it in one arm while he manoeuvres the boat with the other back to the bank. You see the limp chick with bulging eyes which stare with a dreadful resignation. Your father says to you, 'Its neck is broken, love.'

'Will it be all right?' you ask, worried.

'No, love,' he replies honestly. 'It can't get better now.'

He nestles it in sure, knowing hands, holds it low for you to see. Gingerly you reach out and touch the top of its head with your finger. You stroke the dying bird.

Your father propels himself and the chick away again, scowling, past the people who stare but say nothing. Obviously the man is insane bothering with a drowning bird. Into the garden and up the path at the side of the house where we keep the dustbin. Your eyes follow him, but he is careful to keep his back turned.

When he comes back he is empty-handed. He tells you: 'The chick is dead now. It won't suffer any more.'

The Headband is efficient. He is humane. These qualities he passes on to you.

At times like these I would remember the glossy-haired scientist, the mentor, the older man who had wooed me with powerful words and candlelit meals. But recently, coming out of the campus library, I had caught an unexpected glimpse of a middle-aged academic, a man with a luminous headband clamping shoulder-length hair, a man with a threadbare beard and a mauve flowered smock hanging outside his trousers. I hid behind a pillar rather than acknowledge my connection with him.

Finally, it has to be said, simply and plainly and now seems as good a time as any. I took you away from a father you loved. That's the stark fact. Whatever I may think or feel about that man, between the two of you, the chemistry worked just fine.

The Headband supplied you with the facts your mind craved. 'Why, Daddy? Why?' He answered fully and patiently. He filled your young head with a veritable jumble sale of passed-on knowledge and information. He told you why a praying mantis looks like it's praying. He told you how the muscles work in locusts' wings. He told you about the cockroaches he had spent a lifetime studying. It was your father, not me, who brought home a prism and showed you the magic of splintered light. While I cooked supper, he turned your bathtime into a Science Fair, with transparent helter-skelter tubes of water which the pair of you sucked and blew through until the towels were soaked and the floor was awash. He lifted stones in the garden to show you beetles and woodlice. He held a frog in the palm of his hand and showed you how its back legs could stretch and fold, a springboard of energy. He displayed the wonders of his work for you to see, showing off his blue-tinted cells, his red-eyed rats, his scalpels and microscopes, showing you off to everyone else.

And me? I think I gave you my love.

Dear Tom,

You, aged three, had a close and faithful friend next
door, seventy years your senior. I dug my garden, he
dug his garden, and you sat on the wall in between,
compared our produce and kept us company. Old Fred
Lindley really had a soft spot for you, little son of mine.
You knew where to find him, usually in his garden gently
hoeing the soil between his magnificent plants. Why did
mine not grow like his? When he took a break, you
hopped over and joined him on the wall outside his
summer-house. The pair of you – orange juice and
seed-cake amongst the marigolds – and a wonderful,
companionable silence between you. There was no need
for words.

Fred Lindley was champion at bowls. You knew it
because he had silver cups to prove it. For three summers
you watched him hold the reclaimed trophy high above
the fence for you to see. On Tuesdays and Thursdays,
in the late afternoon light, the visiting teams trooped
past our bottom gate and shouted jovially to Fred to
get his skates on and let them into the green. He kept
the keys to the padlock which kept the grounds secure.
You squatted outside the railings, watched the old men
roll the heavy wooden balls. Some mornings Fred would
beckon to you and you would trot at his side up to the
rusting iron gates, knowing he was going to let you,
only you, into the green sanctuary with him. You sat
on a big round stone while Fred mowed fresh stripes
into the already perfect grass.

In the middle of the night you, little one, slept
through the banging on the wall from next door, the
running footsteps, the wail of an elderly stricken wife

and an ambulance siren. But next morning I had to explain that your friend had been taken to hospital.

From the entrance to the ward your wide eyes missed nothing. You took in the rows of beds, the grown men lolling against banks of white pillows, like children tucked up for the night. Except that it wasn't night. A strong summer sun poured in the windows staining the bedspreads with light which was too bright.

Mrs Lindley was at his bedside. She wore a pretty flowered dress and a pearl brooch, but her eyes were pools of sorrow.

'He can't speak,' she whispered. 'But I think he recognises me.'

Your friend's face was suddenly so thin that I could see the shape of the bones beneath the skin. You stared at his twisted, open mouth and the hand that fluttered on the bedspread. Were you reminded of the duckling, I wondered, as I was? You held out the roses we had picked from our garden and he made choking noises in his throat.

I chattered on about our gardens with a dreadful false cheerfulness. I smiled brightly, not knowing how else to behave. After a while Fred made a mighty effort to turn his head so that he could focus on you. The choking noise began again, urgent, determined. Fred Lindley stared down at you and twisted that hand over and back, over and back. We adults froze.

But not you. You climbed up on to the bed beside him and held still his cold, papery hand. You laid your round white face beside his. Fred Lindley was crying, just with his eyes because the rest of his face was paralysed. You clung on. You knew. And slowly, the tears stopped flowing and the rigid body relaxed. We retreated to the bottom of the bed and left the two of you together. In your own way, in the best way anyone possibly could, you said goodbye to your friend.

Later that afternoon, Fred Lindley died. And I was proud of you, my small son, and astonished at what you were able to give him.

Then, when you were young, you had so much to give.

Dear Tom,

The magic of those first summers faded and left me trapped where I thought I would *be* free. Bored with the novelty of encouraging me, The Headband channelled his energies back into his own achievements. Just when I was blossoming myself, he withdrew, leaving me the trivia, the routine, the hassle, the caring. And you. Between the lectures and the thesis, I squeezed full-time mothering into a part-time space. I began to feel the strain of my commitments.

I learnt to dovetail my tasks so as not to waste a single precious moment. In the mornings, between switching on the kettle and waiting for it to boil, I ran my obstacle race. I made the bed, laid the table, fed the cat, scooped up your toys, and sprinted up to wake you. I was a whirling dervish, knowing my thesis and your nursery were waiting, while The Headband moved in slow motion, yawning noisily, lying in the bath and frowning importantly on his day ahead. I pulled on my uniform jeans (no time to think what else to wear), searched for missing papers, trawled beneath the sofa for two shoes, two socks, and ran upstairs, two at a time, to greet you. He sat down to his breakfast, sipped his coffee, collected his thoughts, picked up his briefcase, and walked out to a crisp unruffled morning. He left me his crumbs, his dirty socks, and your tetchiness.

Because recently in the mornings my chirpy bird of a child had become a slow and grumpy snail. There I would be, breathless from all the running up and down, but eager to see your sweet sleepy face on the pillow, pulling back your yellow curtains to let in a stream of bright light, waiting for my reward of your first morning smile. But sometimes I was met with a stiff little body and a cold, blank face.

You watched, while I hopped about your room, dived into drawers, and spread in a row on the carpet, in the right order, your blue vest and pants, your T-shirt, your track suit, and your rescued socks. All right way out and ready for you to step into. A fabric cut-out of my small child. Slowly, slowly, heavy-lidded, you stirred and dangled limp legs from the duvet, lifted your head from the pillow, wormed your way out of bed, all with plain reluctance. So you did not want to leave the lovely warmth of your dreams and your bed, I could sympathise with that. I would hug you, red or green in fleecy pyjamas, and stroke your upside-down nest of hair. I would take you to the window and we would count the birds and watch the water. But only for a moment or two because that was all I could spare. Come on, I would say.

Later, your breakfast sizzling in the frying-pan, I would

return to collect you and find my small statue just where I had left him, a motionless figure at the window, or a seated study of still life with a sock in one hand. So I would pull off your night-clothes and tug on your day ones and down we would go to the smell of fish fingers and the sound of my cheery chatter. Hand in hand we would count the stairs, marching to our morning song, hi ho, hi ho, it's off to work we go. At the table, I hovered, whisking things back into cupboards, willing you to hurry, knowing we were already late, knowing my day was short and my unwritten chapters were waiting. But you were somnolent. Come on, I would urge. You sleep-walked through my chivvyings. Dawdled through my haste. Resisted my attempts to make you move at a normal pace. And I sighed and forgave you because, perhaps, your day did not have the pull of mine. And when at last I had you all licked and polished and bundled up ready to go I was strung up and nervy from the effort it had taken. And my own day had not even begun.

Dear Tom,

Like a punctuation mark at the end of each day, in time for the sherry but not the chores, in time to criticise but not contribute, The Headband would round the bend in the path around the pool. You would wait for him at your bedroom window, race downstairs, run to meet him, often sheltering from my exasperation. Hand in hand, he asked you about your day and told you about his. Outside, you two lingered, watched the birds, watched the pool, watched the skies, watched the easy appreciation on each other's faces. You took your time because it was all your own. Inside I hurried. I stirred pans and washed dishes and tidied away your toys, resentful, envious, because The Headband's day had been better parcelled out than mine. His time less condensed. He had not played 'Beat the Clock', juggling to fit in the work and the chauffeuring and the athletics course around the supermarket in the lunch-hour. Able to slowly weave in his last thoughts as he plodded gently home, he arrived composed, and complacent about what he had got done. If there was steam coming out of my ears because I had been running to stand still and you had dug your heels in, he was smug and scathing. If he returned to tension, he chastised me, pompously, called me emotional, told me sanctimoniously that there were better ways to handle a child. Silently he took your side, entered with you into a conspiracy of understanding that your mother's feathers were more ruffled than they ought, or needed, to be.

Inevitably, he took your side. If you were rude, it was only because you were weary. If you refused to help, it was because my demands were too heavy. If you and I quarrelled, it was because I over-reacted. Not caring to discipline because it was uncomfortable, he opted for the easy route out and took the course of least resistance. Easier to paste over the cracks in your behaviour, to gloss over the problems, than to acknowledge and deal with them. His was the cop-out method of child rearing, the blindfold system of upbringing. That left me the part of ogre and fishwife. He was the parent who always said Yes. So I had to be the one who sometimes said No.

Dear Tom,

The morning tussles went on until they became a routine, so that when you dug in your heels, not to be awkward, but to tell me something, I did not see.

From the start I had been uneasy about the choice of your nursery, had wanted to move you to the other side of town. But The Headband had argued strongly for its convenience, its proximity. Should I be ill, he, Heaven forbid, would have to travel ten miles to deliver and collect you.

And so that terrible landmark of a morning seemed the same as every other. You were a slow motion child. As the hands on the clock ticked on, I watched you grind to an infuriating halt. You chewed more slowly. Gazed into space. Drummed your feet in rhythmic defiance against the side of your chair. You pushed your food around your plate, daring me with sullen glances to try to make you hurry. By eight-fifteen I was anxious. By eight-thirty, desperate. Still you dawdled while I flashed around you collecting up your things. You blocked your ears to requests to search for gloves, to tie up your shoelaces. You made yourself stiff and inert, a lifeless puppet who would not push his own arms down his own anorak sleeves.

And once I had coerced you into the car, you pushed yourself flat against the back of the seat as if the very pressure of your small body could prevent you from being delivered to your nursery. In the back there, strapped into your red car seat, I think you began to perfect that technique of remaining still and quiet and set-faced enough to shut out what was unacceptable in the real world.

Yet, with dreadful inevitability we always arrived, and there was Maggie waiting to clock you in. You didn't like her. You said she had small eyes and fat white legs like maggots. And at mealtimes, she insisted on silence, and pinched bits of food off your plate. Already you objected to eating meat. You said you hated the texture (yes, you knew the word) and chewing it made you feel sick. But vegetarianism wasn't fashionable in those days so you just had to get on with it. Once a week came the dreaded gristly stew.

Maggie would pick you out. 'Hurry up, Tom. We're all waiting for you as usual. Chew and swallow! Chew and swallow!' You learnt to use your cheeks like hamster pouches to hoard the stringy meat until you could spit it out in the garden.

Then, one day another little boy had teeth marks on his hand and you were blamed. Maggie seized you, smacked you and made you stand in a corner. Torture of torture, you could hear Mr Men on the telly but couldn't see the pictures because your back was turned. That was how I found you on that one fortuitous occasion when I decided to push aside my books earlier than usual and collect you. Maggie had asked you to admit that you had bitten the other child. You had denied it. Over and over again. Rather than own up to something you had not done, you stuck it out. Rather than make peace. I pushed open the front door of the shabby old building just in time to hear Maggie shouting, 'You're a nasty little boy. A very nasty little boy indeed!'

That was the last time you went there. I grabbed you and your green anorak and your blue shoe-bag with the capital 'T' embroidered on it and told you with my arms tight around you that you would never go back.

Or is it just within the bounds of possibility that you could be a stubborn little brute even then? I talk from experience, remember. Did you drive Maggie to the point of cruelty?

Were you really a very nasty little boy?

Dear Tom,

That last summer, thank God, the pressure eased. My thesis was all but written and only the final sprint remained. Just as well. For when the sun shone and the days lengthened, I could not work. Like a tortoise, I emerged from my shell and went in search of warmth. I had spent nine months rushing and fractured, frantic and fierce. Now I could grow calm again. From July to September, guiltily, I threw my papers to the wind and sank my hands deep into the earth.

My body craved fresh air and sunlight and crumbly soil. My fingers itched to prod holes for new cuttings torn from old wood, to poke bits of thyme and lavender into the warming ground. I could not wait to roll up my sleeves and get down to the wonderful, grubby, earthy business of weeding and hoeing and planting. I wanted to be left in peace to crouch down in my flower-beds, my bare arms and legs smudged with soil and my face turned up to the sun. I wanted to put down my own roots as you were putting down yours.

For you it was a happy time. A time in a world which was safe and known. You were a free spirit roaming round the pool and gazing at the circle of water. You explored the dark alleys between the terraced houses and you made a map in your head of the place where you lived. You knew where to find the clumps of orange flowers with leaves like reeds. You knew where the foxes lived beneath the bowling pavilion in the hollow of dark, crumbling earth. You knew to take a wide berth round the high-hedged gardens where dogs snarled and mad old Gertie shouted rude enticements to invisible lovers. You knew not to stray too near the water. You knew who to run to if you needed help. I sensed the day-dreams which crowded your head and was glad that you had time to watch them. You knew the choices which each day brought and you knew the routines which divided up the hours. Your skin turned brown in the sun and the wind, and your hair grew like pale straw. I loved you so.

But you were aware of cracks appearing in the rose-coloured picture. You had tuned into your parents' tension and your term-time days had made you afraid.

I sensed a watching, an uneasiness in you. Sometimes I felt you following me with dissatisfied eyes; I sensed you clinging to me like a sad limpet. Why, I wondered, when you had so many places to explore, did you need to trail around listlessly after me? Why did you place yourself, like a wedge, silent and determined, between me and anything else I wanted to do? Why, when you had all that space, could you not leave me some of my own? You would hover over me, constantly, until I was forced to sit back on my heels, push back a sticky lock of hair and dump my armful of uprooted vegetation.

'Hello, Tom.'

'What are you doing?'

'Weeding. You can see that I'm weeding. What do you want?' I would look at your mournful little face and try to *will* the irritation out of my voice.

'Will you play a game with me?'

The dreaded request. I had pushed you in swings, read stories and made Playdoh. I had looked at catalogues and taken you for walks and taught you to read. I had watched cartoons and hidden in cupboards and jumped on trampolines. Now I wanted some time for myself.

'No. Not now.'

'Why not?'

'Because I want to do this.'

You, a persistent child in the face of plain discouragement, were not that easily beaten. 'Can I help?'

We both knew what that meant. But, ever guilty at the amount of time I spent with my head buried in my papers, sending off silent signals to you to keep away, I usually gave in. Mums who devote the whole day to being a taxi-driver and cooking gingerbread men and making clothes for teddies have a right to say No. I didn't.

So, resigned, I showed you what was weed and what was grass and what was delphinium and suggested you clear a little patch like I was doing around the plants. You crouched next to me and tugged up one, perhaps two, blades of grass and then sat there with the corners of your mouth pulled down, staring at me. Obstinate.

Critical. Willing me to stop. Pulling me away from what I was absorbed in. Wanting me to devote myself only to you.

'What's the matter?'

'Don't want to garden. It's too hot.'

'What do you want to do?'

'I want you to play a game with me.'

'Look, I've only got this bit to finish. Please, I just want to clear this bit of ground and get the last of these little plants in, and then I'll come and play with you. Okay?'

No, it wasn't okay. You continued to sit there, picking at the grass. The picture of neglect. Sometimes a tear would roll down your cheek. And in the end either I lost my temper and told you to go away and play on your own, or, worse, gave in to your demands and joined in some mind-numbing game with very bad grace.

And this before the fighting began. This before you ran to the pool to block your ears against our shouting. This before you sensed the plotting and scheming which was to pull out the roots of your own solid foundations.

Dear Tom,

Our lives are made up of little things – courtesies, acknowledgements, success, respect. We can't go on without them. Your father's ego was fed from rich sources and his confidence never wavered. But I, belittled by his arrogance, faltered.

Winter and summer The Headband carried his black

briefcase to and from work. And on holiday. And to visit friends. The briefcase was his emblem. His reminder to all of us of his self-importance. It defined him. It sustained his status and his arrogance. Even on weekend visits to his parents, the briefcase came too. We would spend a jolly evening discussing his next conference and his cancerous cockroaches and his latest triumphs. He could have put in a word for me. In that brochure home of cut glass and correct cutlery, where you and I lived in dread of marking the dining-table with a ring of Ribena or treading mud into the carpet of wall-to-wall silver, he could have let them know that he found something of value in me, even if they didn't.

Instead, there I was in the last throes of writing my thesis, full of vulnerability, eagerness, enthusiasm, and not allowed to express them. Not even allowed to be tired.

'Ask your mother not to wake us up in the morning, will you? I'm tired out, looking after Tom and finishing my thesis. I don't like her barging in here, flinging open the curtains as if we were kids at boarding-school, for Heaven's sake. And in full flight when I haven't even got my eyes open. Cocktail chatter at seven-fifteen! It's not on.'

'Oh, it's not important, surely?'

'But I want to sleep in. Or, at least wake up in my own time. She doesn't even knock!'

'She never has! It's just her way.'

'Tell her! I don't want her charging in on us first thing in the morning. I want some privacy. I do not want to be talked at when I am not even awake!'

'Oh look, we're only here for three days so it's just not worth the fuss.'

I got the message. Never mind if I needed to sleep more than anything else in the world. If he were exhausted it would have been different. But my work did not count, did not even register. So I continued to be rudely awakened and my work remained unacknowledged. By tea-time on the first day, I had vanished into the tasteful wallpaper.

I wondered if The Headband had any idea what it was like to dovetail a dozen different tasks so as not to waste a single useful moment. Or did it suit him not to know, not to recognise the impossibility of my days as I drove you to your nursery, answered your incessant questions, soothed your anxiety, made sure you had what you needed, endured your clinging parting, and raced to start work with a sinking heart. Worked through the lunch-hour so you could be collected early. Stopped mid-sentence to race to get to you on time. Dragged around the shops at the end of a busy day and picked up the mess and cleaned the toilet and froze the *coq au vin* in case important visiting speakers came. Made a commitment to turn my mind round a hundred and eighty degrees at three-thirty prompt each day to become a mum, and only a mum, for you.

Sometimes, harassed, trying to hang on to some half-formed idea which had been cut off by the clock, I would plead with him, 'Could you collect Tom tomorrow and let me work late?' or 'Please could you take just one afternoon off and help me sort out the spare room.'

(For 'the spare room' please substitute at random

'the allotment', 'the visiting in-laws', 'the empty freezer' or 'my pile of computer print-out which I cannot decipher'.)

'Look, I'm afraid it's out of the question. There's a meeting in Dublin next week.'

(For 'a meeting in Dublin' please substitute at random 'a visiting speaker from Iceland', 'a new lecturer starting in the department' or 'an important paper that has to be finished.')

But let's get it into perspective. I was only a post-graduate student; he was a renowned scientist.

But then The Headband's work was mysterious and thrilling to a three-year-old child. Down in the bowels of the basement there was a peep-show, a theatre, a fair-ground of attractions. Riding high on his shoulders, you toured the stalls, the test-tubes of minced matter, the blue-dyed cells, the containers of crusty cockroaches, the rabbits with albino eyes, the students with pipettes in their mouths. And all the time The Headband talking, explaining, talking.

On Fridays we would collect The Headband early *en route* from your nursery. It was his one concession. We would hover in his room while he packed his briefcase to his own insistent commentary.

'Right. I must re-draft that letter to the Dean and I'd better take that chapter home to work on. Then there's the Durham meeting next week. Did I tell you Martin's going to give a paper. . .'

'Yes, you did tell me.'

'Look Daddy,' you chipped in, perhaps sensing the tension between us. You were perched on a lab-stool with a big, heavy calculator, engrossed in your own entertainment. 'I've written two thousand two hundred and fifty.' You pointed insistently at the flickering red numbers.

'Good boy!' The Headband pronounced. 'Those are called digits, can you remember that?'

His way of talking to you was driving me insane. Our child was neither retarded nor partially deaf. He could by now follow the cadences of ordinary spoken English. Nor was it necessary at every opportunity to drill him in numeracy, science and environmental studies before he had even started school.

'Can we please go!' I snapped. 'I've been standing in this doorway for fifteen minutes and I'm very tired.'

'Then sit down for Christ's sake. Don't be a spoil-sport. We'll only be a minute.'

It wasn't only a minute. It was another thirty minutes. On you two went, tapping in numbers, while he lectured at you in pedantic staccato. If ever, Heaven forbid, he were made redundant, he could get a job training parrots to talk. Defeated, I put down my work-laden basket, and closed my eyes in sheer exhaustion.

A long time later, on the way out to the car, I felt the soft rain on my face and felt like weeping. The Headband drove. You waved crumpled sheets of sugar-paper between us. Still craving attention. The Headband released a hand from the wheel and accepted your offering of dried pasta and paste, squinting at it each time we passed under a lamppost. Talking in a voice turned up too loud as if he had forgotten he was no longer in the lecture hall.

'It is excellent! I cannot see it very well but I will look at it when we get home.'

'There are wheels and shells and spirals. . .'

'Good boy! Well done! And that is a hexagon, isn't it? And this one with five sides, do you know what this is called?'

On you two went again. On and on and on. The light from the street-lamps flashed on and off as we drove under them. I leant my face against the cold glass and let the tears fall. Against the streaming window pane no one noticed.

Dear Tom,

I am trying to give you a truthful account of those first years when you were small and the seasons changed and I sank my hands deep into the soil. But I know that the angle is mine.

Your early roots ran deep and were tough, tough to pull out and move to fresh ground. No wonder you dug your heels in.

One day, the last day of The Headband's absence at a conference, I realised I could not go on. It sounds a sudden thought, but it wasn't. Like when you see something through a mist and you stare and stare trying to make it out, then suddenly the mist clears and there it is. Clear as a bell. I woke that morning, alone in the double bed, and as I stretched my body luxuriously into the empty half and my mouth into a real, big smile, I realised how gloriously glad I was that The Headband wasn't there.

Today there would be no struggle to rouse him from his weekend inertia. There would be no frowning figure slumped on the sofa, no limp presence sipping coffee behind reams of text. You and I would not plead with him to be ready, pace the pavement, watch grimly while the sun faded and vanished. We would not wait and wait and wait while he read *New Scientist* in the bath.

Today I would not be put down by his loud monologues or stifled by his talk fit for lecture halls, not living-rooms. I would not be steam-rollered by his scathing, arrogant intellect. I would not be reduced to frustrated silence at the dinner-table because he corrected my assumptions, finished my sentences and sabotaged my stories. I was free to speak, and it was wonderful to find my voice again.

That day, I felt as if someone had cut the ropes which held me down and allowed me to float away free. I had sprouted wings and found a lightness of being. I did not want him to come home.

You may remember that day because I pushed you in your striped buggy round and round the block, up and down the streets, through the park and back, for hour after hour, wondering what on earth to do. I probably wasn't much company. Maybe I asked you not to talk to me, saying I was tired. Maybe I answered you in monosyllables, while my mind was elsewhere. In the time it took your father to land at the airport and get in the car and drive home, I had made up my mind.

On we walked, for miles, and as we went, you kicking bare legs and pulling bits out of the hedgerows, I tried to see it all another way round and couldn't. As I pushed your buggy, the wheels turned and I thought about your childhood, about myself travelling such a long long way through it, growing and changing and becoming wiser, and all the time The Headband had stood still.

I knew that I had come to the end of the road. I knew I could not stick it out much longer. I wondered whether to hare back there and then and pack our bags and run away before he arrived home because I did not want him in the same house, in the same bed, in the same space any more. I remember I sat down on the kerb and rested my head on my hands.

You asked, 'What's the matter, Mummy?' and I couldn't tell you.

If I left, you would have to leave with me, because I was the one who looked after you. I believed I was the one you needed most. To leave you behind was not an option. Then, when you were three years old, I could not live without you.

Two more circuits round the block and I had come to a decision. This had to be thought out. Planned out. Instead of running away, it must be done rationally, with honest explanations and civilised decisions. On the surface your life should continue undisturbed while The Headband and I worked out your future.

But, of course, it wasn't like that. The anger boiled over and it was impossible to hide it from you. When the yelling broke out you ran for cover. You ran outside, pressing your hands to your ears. Once, after we two had hurled abuse and plates at each other's heads, I went upstairs to find you crouched on the floor at the bottom of your bed, frozen like an animal in a car's headlights.

I know it was awful for you.

When it finally came, you turned your face against the change with a cold, passive determination never to be a part of it. How much silent protest and power can a four-year-old exert! One day I packed you and my plants and my sewing machine into the car and drove away for ever. You were squeezed into the back seat between the bedding and the red geranium. Given that I was taking away your father's most treasured possession, it was hardly fair to take much else. I left our house intact. I watched you in my rear mirror, all the way to Bristol, your gold silk hair a perfect pudding bowl mop and your whole face a perfect frown.

Part 2: Single mother, single son

Dear Tom,

We both found it hard, very hard, living in Eva's house in Bristol. Sharing the same entrance, using her staircase to reach our rooms above, we felt like flies caught in a web. Beneath us our lonely spider of a landlady listened for our footsteps, monitored our comings and goings, and for her sport trapped single mums with heavy shopping bags or stacks of computer print-out, and little children exhausted from long days at nursery school. We tried to sneak across the hall but the soles of our shoes scratched in the cord matting; we tried to creep up the single flight of stairs but the creaking wood of the bare steps gave us away. In any case she was waiting for us, listening for the sound of the key turning in the front door. She only wanted a friend, and I, a wrung-out single mum, wanted only to be left alone.

Uphill, I found it. Uphill to the shops and the launderette and the park where you wanted to play. Uphill with arms pulled out of their sockets, laden with bags at the end of the day. Uphill against your resentment and unhappiness. Coming back at four or five or six, I would lean my load against the banisters while Eva chatted brightly about her day, relieved to have someone to tell it to. I edged up one step at a time, sliding the carrier-bags or the piles of damp clothing up the staircase rail. Sometimes it took us ten minutes, sometimes twenty, to reach the top. You sighed long and hard, narrowed your eyes and cast me desperate looks, willing me to have the courage or the honesty to protest. Like piggy-in-the-middle, I jumped first to her demands, then to yours. Alternately, a plastic smile for her, a look of concern and a pat on the shoulder for you. What else could I do? Defeated by small talk, you would curl up like a foetus on one of the stairs with your golden head hanging down between the struts. Often, often, you complained that her voice pushed out of your head all the things you had been waiting to tell me. But at last, when she had gone, and I dumped my bags and knelt down ready to listen to you, you were sullen and silent behind our closed door.

But even there, we were not safe. Cooking smells – garlic and onions and ginger – heralded the inevitable knock on the door and an offer too generous to refuse. 'I've made some lovely carrot and coriander soup. Will you both come down and have a bite with me? Or shall I put some in a pan for you? I can bring it up if you would prefer. It will do you both good. You look pale, my dear. And much too thin.'

Of course I was thin. I was thin from skipping meals, bolting meals because I was in a hurry, thin from worrying, thin from trying to give you something at the end of the day when I had nothing in reserve. Thin from pushing you on your bike and skipping with you in the park and swimming with you in the pool, when all I wanted was to close my eyes and sleep.

Of course I was pale. Pale from burning the candle at both ends because there was no one else to lighten the burden. Pale from the fraud of staring at Jimbo and Mr Men, for your sake, while I puzzled out what to do with our lives. Pale from the effort of trying to be calm and steady and kind with a difficult child because I had forfeited the right to be bad-tempered. Pale from coping single-handed with a new job and a small boy who would not be pleased, no matter what I did, and who drained every ounce of nervous energy from me. Pale from having no time or space to call my own. Pale from the guilt of knowing I had made you wretched.

I hated the flat with its cold north light, and so did you. From the high windows, a view of roof-tops and drainpipes had replaced the pool and the foxes. Your riot of toys and paintings had been replaced by a single dark bookcase, which I stacked with games and books and which you left alone. Instead of your bunk-beds, a stiff old divan. Instead of sun and wind and freedom, electric radiators and heavy sighs. I did my best. I painted the sludge-green walls of your bedroom a bright yellow like fake sunshine, and I pinned posters of foxes around your bed. But the look on your face every bedtime chastised me, these were no substitute for the real thing.

One week was much like the rest. Both of us sleepily silent in the mornings, knowing my work and your nursery school were our inevitable deadlines. You protected yourself with private thoughts and images which clung like gossamer webs, and walked through my brisk routines in dreamlike sequences.

My work was as dreary and as dry as dust. In a grimy room at the very top of a gloomy tenement overlooking traffic, I decoded holes in yellow punch cards. The room filled up with computer print-out and I slowly sank in four-by-four tables. I shuffled and reshuffled the punctured cards. Most days I wondered what I was doing there.

Thank goodness, you fared better. Behind the 'Welcome' sign on your nursery school door, there was fun and colour and laughter, a place where children grew watercress and baked bread and tended hamsters. Across the other side of town. Through traffic and fumes and cross drivers and uncrossable junctions. An enormous detour, but I did not want you anywhere else.

But, even there, you found it hard to settle. That first day, and every day after for two whole terms, you clung to my neck and twisted your legs around mine so that I could not walk away from you. Mrs May unwound your limbs and gently prised us apart. She signalled for me to leave while she held her arms around you and patiently talked you out of your panic. She hung on to you until you stopped struggling and allowed yourself to be tempted by a story or the cars on the ramp or the beans waiting to be planted. Every morning she put aside a chunk of precious time to deal with your terrors. She understood that you had already lost your father and you were afraid of losing your mother as well. And after school, when all the other children had gone home, you stayed behind and helped Mrs May lift up the chairs and feed the hamster and put out the games ready for the next day. When all was done, she drove you to my work, or took you home with her for juice and biscuits or a walk in the park with her shaggy dog. She understood the plight we were in. Without her, I don't know what we would have done.

In clement weather you spilled out into a playground of suspended tyres, swinging ropes and working wooden trucks with steering-wheels which turned. On the grass verge, Fred the tortoise and Sooty, the rabbit with velvet fur. In the middle, a space-age concoction of child-sized tubes, orange ladders and hidden capsules which took you to the moon and back before the bell went.

Your teacher wore a necklace of wooden beads which one of the children had made for her. They offered her gifts of daisy-chains and Playdoh rings and loving smiles. She was something out of a fairy-tale. They fought to hold her hand, to sit on her knee, to plant their sticky kisses on her cheeks.

One Monday morning you were hysterical because The Headband had been, and had gone again. You fought like a wild thing, kicking and biting and digging your nails into Mrs May's flesh while she held you hard. I turned my back and walked out on your sobs and your crying. I drove to work with my hands shaking on the wheel. In the mirror, your grief-stricken face, and above the roar of traffic, your screams.

And so I invented games to drag you through your troubled days. Do you remember the flyover game we played on the way back from school? Anything to get a response from that sad little face. It was an insane game to play with a child. Right in the middle of town, where the traffic flowed fast and furious and the roads wound above and below each other in a tangled mileage of concrete, I would slow down on the slip-road, wait for a gap in the stream of cars, then turn round to you, sitting silently on the back seat.

'Right, this is where you get out. Off you go then. See you tomorrow.'

Your mouth would twitch with the hint of a smile. You would crouch down on the floor behind the driving seat, waiting for the next move. In the midst of life in an unnerving state of flux, you loved this predictable game

'Good, he's gone. I've had quite enough of him for one day. Now for a bit of peace and quiet.'

On cue, you popped up again. By now we were speeding along the dual carriageway as the road curved round to meet the flyover.

'Oh no!' I shouted crossly. 'Not still here. Out you get! I've already told you I've had enough of you.'

In my mirror I watched you bob down again between the seats. Your knees and elbows stuck through the worn fabric of my seat into my back. We roared up on to the flyover until the cars below looked like crawling ants. You held your breath as we bounced over the hump in the road and whizzed down the other side. Up you popped again, and on we sped, me still yelling at you to jump out. I always drove too fast in Bristol. Always late. Always tense. Always in a breathless headlong hurry.

What a dumb game. What a bloody stupid game to invent for a four-year-old kid. For all I knew, you might have taken me at my word. Then one night you woke screaming because in a nightmare you had jumped and been crushed beneath the wheels of other cars and I had not even noticed your absence. You sobbed that I did not even stop the car to find out if you were dead or alive. I had just carried on driving.

Dear Tom,

Do you remember how you were convinced that every tunnel we drove through on our journeys to and from school housed a dragon? Bristol is full of tunnels. The bigger the tunnel, the bigger the dragon. It stands to reason. We would toot the horn to alert the dragon we were coming, debating as to its exact whereabouts in the damp, gloomy darkness, and swerve wildly to avoid its breath of fire.

Then, one day, I drove right into the bloody stone wall. Probably I had slept badly, had woken in the early hours to lie worrying. About you. I should have kept my bleary eyes on the road, and told you there was no game that day, but the dragons kept your mind off the nursery, and sometimes saved me from your tears. Our battered Citroën Diane was wedged by its bumper, impaling us, right in the dragon's lair. You yelled with delight at the delay, and faked terror that we would be burnt to cinders. I was much more alarmed about jamming up a dark, narrow tunnel in the middle of the rush-hour.

Someone must have raised the alarm because a police car turned up fairly rapidly and sealed off both entrances with diversion signs. And you, gleeful at this new move in our game, actually told the officer that we had been swerving to avoid the dragon. He was not amused. He lifted his pen from his notepad and told you, sonny, to let your mother do the explaining. You flashed daggers at me when I reported that the car must have slipped on a wet patch on the road. Sorry, I was dishonest. I let you down. But you had to learn that busy policemen do not want to know about the fiery dragons that live in the Bristol tunnels.

All the time we were there, I was wound up like a spring. Coiled up tight with anxiety. I managed to have three accidents in nine months. Thank God only the car got damaged.

One dreadful jump-started morning, when you needed to cling and I needed to get to work, I had to drag you down Eva's stairs. You sat moodily in the car, working yourself up to your pre-nursery misery, as the rain streamed down the windscreen. The engine chose that moment to splutter to a choking full stop. For you it was a diversion, a welcome delay to your day. Cheery for the first time in weeks, you started chanting mumbo-jumbo, shouting car-starting spells. But I had been late three times already that week, and my heart sank. I was tired. I was exasperated. Pumping the pedal, I willed the bloody thing to start.

'Shut up!' I shouted over my shoulder. 'Will you shut up! I can't hear a thing.'

Grimly, you continued, drumming a refrain, making it more difficult than it already was, blocking the slimmest chance of success.

'Right, get out. Go on, get out. Help me push it back up the hill. I'll have to jump start it.'

You climbed reluctantly into the rain. But we couldn't budge the car an inch.

The rain trickled down my neck and through my thin gloves and through the holes in the soles of my boots. Three boys wandered past on their way to school and were rapidly coerced into helping. Between us we heaved and shunted the car up the hill, our shoulders against the bonnet. 'Right, look out, everyone! I'm going to jump in! Get out of the way, Tom! Stay out of the way.'

I ran alongside the car for a few yards, hanging on to the open door, but the car gathered momentum and I could not keep up with it. I tried to get one foot on to the floor of the driving seat and ended up being dragged at a crazy gallop downhill. I was lucky to stumble back against the pavement rather than be caught under the wheels. Three boys in school uniform, and one small one without, cheered and jeered as a wet, wild, weeping woman tore downhill after a runaway car. I watched as the car crashed into a wall. One wreck watching another.

I lived on a knife-edge. Spiky and tense, I battled against your torpid resistance. I would do anything, almost anything, to raise a smile on your little white face.

So when you came home from nursery, carrying a tray full of stick-insects, I stoically kept my mouth shut. What other pets could we smuggle past The Spider's beady eyes? I had smashed the car, repeatedly, dropped every fragile pot in the house, and now feared all those living, breakable arms and legs, those masses of skinny, detachable limbs. Slowly, carefully, we decanted them from newspaper to jam-jars, and you were satisfied. They were yours, and you named the biggest one George. For a few weeks you contentedly stuck leaves and wet blobs of cotton wool into their transparent home.

And then, one day, they escaped. The wretched leggy things got out of their glass and muslin prisons and walked about all over my kitchen. I trod on one. There were two in the sink. Their legs came off. Despite your pleas not to panic, I did. Seizing the muslin with insects still attached I heaved up the sash-window and shook them out. They wouldn't budge. That did it. You ran for cover while I gathered up jars, muslin, dishcloths, anything likely to conceal stick-insects and hurled the lot out of the window. We were on the second floor, remember, and when the glass crashed to the concrete slabs twenty feet below, I half hoped I had managed to murder the Black Widow at the same time.

Poor Tom. You wept. You sat under the kitchen table and howled for your stick-insects. For weeks afterwards we kept finding them. One turned up alive, clinging to the top shelf (you were convinced it was George) and there was a dead one, legs up in the cutlery drawer.

For days and weeks you scowled at me and punished me with your furious silence.

Dear Tom,

One day, after your fourth birthday, I told you an old friend was coming to see me. I said it was someone I hadn't seen for a very long time. You must have known. Those emotional antennae of yours wavered in the breeze and picked up my change of mood. You watched your mum bounce up the stairs two at a time, a gleam in her eye, roses in her cheeks. You stared as I fussed over beef in red wine. When I told you to hurry and eat up your fish fingers you put down your fork in silent protest.

Watchful, you perched silently on the edge of the

bath while I slipped on a rich silk blouse, smudged my eyes with kohl-black circles. Vigilant, you gazed as I unwound and shook out my long hair. You picked up my heady scent, my delirious hope, my excitement. Perhaps you saw that I was remaking myself, painting over the haggard single mum, and drawing back in the woman. Perhaps you guessed that this man I waited for with trembling hands and smiling mouth was no run-of-the-mill visitor. Already, before he came, I think you felt that he was some kind of threat. Sitting there, still and silent, you judged me, and drew your battle lines.

When the doorbell rang, I jumped. I told you sharply to stay where you were. Told you I wanted to answer the door alone. I was greedy to have him all to myself. But you followed me to the top of the stairs, squeezed your head between the wooden struts of the banisters, made sure you did not miss one moment of the drama. You saw me trip and stumble in my nervousness, saw me crash clumsily against the wall as I rushed downstairs. You saw me run with quick steps and glowing eyes across the rough cord matting. You saw me pause to close my eyes and take a deep calming breath before I opened the door.

And there he was on the doorstep, a towering stranger in a torn tatty anorak, bringing a huge bear hug and a flood of memories past. He held my gaze and kneaded his firm hands into my knotted shoulders. My heart pounded. The blood raced through my veins and into my cheeks. I remembered. I remembered feelings which had been buried for so many years.

Somehow you were there, at our side, looking up

at this man who must have seemed a giant. You were there, pushing between us, pushing us apart.

'You must be Tom,' Jim said, letting me go, giving you his full attention, bending down to shake your hand. 'It's very nice to meet you.'

It was then that you noticed that his hands were black with sump oil and that he had smudges of grime down one cheek. His car had broken down.

Bending down again to you, he asked, 'Do you by any chance have a piece of string I can borrow so that I can tie up the fan belt? Would you like to help me?'

One quick glance at my face to check my willingness and you were off, back upstairs to find the string and out into the night with your anorak and wellies over your pyjamas. And off you trotted, your arm stretched up taut so that you could reach the tall stranger's hand.

And so you welcomed the funny stranger who arrived out of the blue that night. You returned from your first outing together with hands as black as his and a grin from ear to ear.

'His car's all battered!' you whispered as I wiped the grease from your fringe and urged you to concentrate on brushing your teeth. 'It's worse than ours. Much worse. He's got a really old Ford Cortina and it's all rusty. One door is tied on with wire and I had to hold the bonnet open while he mended the fan belt. He said he has to use quite a lot of string to make it go!' You giggled behind your hand, an almost forgotten gesture. Yes, at first you accepted the restless, gangling stranger who made old cars start and threw you in the air and dangled you by your feet. But when Jim's arm strayed around your mother's shoulders, or when our eyes met for too long, you drew back, troubled.

Very early the next morning Jim dragged a duvet into the lounge to make an unconvincing nest of bedding on the floor. I followed with the pillows. Your bedroom door was open a crack, as always, and when I peeped in you were still asleep. At least your eyes were closed. But moments later, too soon for coincidence, you padded across the hall and stood, sullen, sad, beside my bed. When I reached out to hug you my arms stayed empty.

'What's the matter, love?' I asked.

'Nothing,' you said.

A small boy in red pyjamas, you positioned yourself at my side in hostile, silent accusation. I sensed puzzlement. I sensed fear and I didn't know what to tell you. And at breakfast you barely acknowledged the stranger who the previous night had been your friend.

Dear Tom,

You have to admit Jim tried. And he went on trying for years. He built stools so you could reach the table, and showed you ships in Bristol Docks. For you he unlocked his vast storehouse of knowledge about winds, tides, currents and boats. He taught you the ropes until you made a fine second-mate yourself. I have a photo of you standing gale-swept but satisfied beside a colossal windbreak of sea-flung detritus on a bare sandy beach. At first you had rejected Jim's offer of a day out for the lads. You said, it was all mud at Weston-super-Mare with no rock-pools where you could search for sea creatures. You turned down the corners of your mouth, and shook your head. Perhaps it was the suggestion of fish and chips and a pint of beer for lunch which persuaded you in the end to go.

It was gusting Force Eight and your hair blew in streamers. At first you tried to make sand-castles with an orange plastic mould, but the wind raged straight along the beach blowing the sand into your eyes. Then, apparently, Jim walked off and left you. You reported he vanished, leaving you squatting alone in the gale. You thought he had dumped you.

Then, at last, he reappeared, rolling a huge battered oil drum and carrying several broken fence posts. Alarm gave way to incredulity as you brushed away your tears and asked, 'What are you going to do with them?'

'What do you think?' he teased. Without expanding further, he stood the barrel on its end and, with a rock which must have weighed a ton, drove the gateposts deep into the sand.

'Come and help me roll that log,' he said, dragging you away with him. 'What we need is a windbreak.'

So that was it. To give him his due, he was full of surprises, but you had not yet got used to them. With you at his side, Jim rolled and pushed and tugged the log along the beach to your embryo construction. Then you braced yourselves again against the gale and tracked along the tideline searching for timber and corrugated iron and debris thrown up by the sea. You couldn't talk much because the wind blotted out the words. The wind took away your breath and you worked in silence alongside each other. You worked all morning, leaning against that perishing wind, but at last you were proud and smiling and satisfied.

'Now we can get on with the sand-castles,' you announced at the end of the three hours' sweated labour. 'After all it does shelter us from the wind.'

You crouched down once more with the orange mould as the first raindrops made black spots on the grey sand.

'But not the rain,' Jim said. 'Quick, Tom, stand there and let me take a picture, before we get soaked.' He unwrapped his camera from the insides of his anorak and snapped your approving face.

The heavens opened and the rain blew in horizontal sheets until your hair clung to your head in flat, wet ribbons. Jim grabbed your hand and you both ran as fast as your short legs would carry you to the different shelter of the nearest pub. You ate fish and chips while your cheeks burned from the wind and your eyes glowed with excitement.

Yet afterwards, when you reached home and I asked you how your day was, your mood lapsed again into sullenness. You pressed your back into the sofa and sealed your lips tight against my cheerful probings.

Dear Tom,

How did I expect you to cope? Did I really hope for jolly adaptation on your part as your own father and a surrogate one popped up on alternate weekends like the fine and wet weather figures that trundle out of

Grandpa's old clock?

On Thursday evenings you took to asking morosely, 'Who's coming tomorrow, my daddy, or Jim?'

Weekends of loyal companionship with your father were followed with appalling regularity by others when you were wedged miserably between your mother and the man who was stealing her away. The man who would have given you the world, if you had let him.

Meanwhile Jim and I were picking up the threads of an old old friendship and slowly knitting them back together. Often, after we had parted, so many years ago, I used to dream of a long line of men marching silently past me. Like soldiers, they turned towards me as they drew level, and I looked into their faces. I would tremble, grow cold and desperate, because none of them were his. He was gone, and I would wake in floods of tears. Now it took only days, maybe only hours, before I knew that in all the space between then and now I had never been able to replace him. I began to tug at the past to make it meet the present. I could not tell you any of this. I could not tell you how I had longed for this man, only this man, to come into my life again.

Once a fortnight he came. He drove six hundred miles to bring us his energy and his love. He was persistent. He was patient. He listened, and helped and cared for us both. He came with bottles of good red wine and strong reliable hands which mended cars and carried shopping. And reached out to touch me. To hug me. To take my hand in his. He arrived on Eva's doorstep with a look in his eyes and a rhythm in his breathing which told me how much he wanted me. Those Friday nights, we watched one another, waited until you were fast asleep. Then we lost ourselves in our old-new passion.

Those weekends kept me going, Tom. I could not have done without them. The other days were ticked off and discarded, incomplete and empty without him.

One sharp blue morning, one of many when Jim and I took refuge from prying eyes in the beautiful woods near Clifton, we came across an oak lying across our path, straddling a dip scooped out of the land. The early sun lit bright spots on the reddish undergrowth, and the air smelt of spring. Hand in hand, we sat and squirmed our toes in the leaf-mould. Such pleasure again in simple things.

You were restless, kicking at the tree, chipping away at our closeness.

'Come on then,' Jim capitulated, 'bet you can't balance on it!'

At the other end of the log he swung you up, steadied your stiff body until your mouth offered the ghost of a smile. He held you until you could balance without wobbling. Then he came back to me, leaving you alone. We threaded our fingers, whispered our plans and promises. I leant my head on his shoulder.

Your whining voice broke into our stillness. You were moaning that you might fall. I glanced back and saw through your eyes, your mother soft and mellow against this man's shoulder. I pictured the closeness you saw.

You created a moment of perfect balance. Your will against my need. Your need willing me away from a man who had come between us. You looked at me, and I looked back, and slowly, inevitably, you started to wobble. I saw your pain but felt my own resentment.

My anger. Knew I should go to you, my damaged child. Knew I shouldn't. Knew I should sit through your childish emotional blackmail. In uncanny slow motion, you lurched from side to side while I watched, until finally you plunged headlong into an enormous clump of nettles.

A switch clicked and in automatic mother-mode I ran to rescue you. With strained grace, I found dock leaves, and rubbed at the white blobs on your back and the palms of your hands. Dried your tears. Sat in the damp grass with my arm around you. I kept my back to Jim, conscious in every bone of my body, that he was standing, shrugging on his anorak, thrusting hands into pockets, and walking slowly away.

Dear Tom,

In the cold early dawns of those weekend mornings, we would wake to the sound of creaking floorboards as you made your inevitable way across the landing. With icy feet and an icy heart you shuffled on your bottom and positioned yourself like a small sentry outside our bedroom door. Always at some ungodly hour before the birds had begun to sing.

'Go back to bed,' I called, knowing you were there.

'Can I come in?' you would whisper plaintively.

'No. It's much too early. Go back to bed.'

'I don't want to go back to bed.'

Whatever I said, whatever I did, you stayed outside our door. You would hug your knees and rock backwards and forwards on the scratchy carpet. Our door would inch open a twinge further, then a twinge further still. I would hold my breath, my eyes closed tight, refuse to look at you, while every beat of my heart shot sharp little images of you on to my retina, a small, cold, wretched child watching the two of us together in the big warm bed.

But Jim, like me feigning sleep, had had enough. 'Tom, go away!' he bellowed. 'Go away! Do you understand? The longer you sit out there the longer we shall be. It's too early.'

Then the sighs would become sniffs and the sniffs sobs and a small boy hurled himself into the room, his face crumpled and his cheeks damp with tears. Jim rolled over on his side, his face turned away from you. He pulled the covers over his head in disgust. I held you in my arms and rubbed your frozen hands and feet, but what good could I do? You were waiting for this stranger to go away and leave us alone again.

Dear Tom,

We stuck it out for a while longer but my days grew hollow, my job pointless, and the separation from Jim too hard to bear. Through a bleak autumn, I paced the Bristol streets, grey-faced and shivering in the cold, frozen in a state of indecision. I knew what I wanted. As I walked through dead leaves, I persuaded myself that you would cope with the changes I plotted. That we would win you round.

When we left Bristol it was with a new father, bound

for a new home, and your small round face turned a whiter shade of pale.

We moved back, close to your old roots, too close for comfort so that you could be within visiting distance of The Headband, just like the textbooks said. We went to an anonymous street of dull terrace houses; our home a half-way house between the past and a future we hadn't worked out yet.

You became a carrier-bag child, a boy with ready-packed pyjamas, toothbrush, and wellies, in case it rained. Your belongings stood ready in the hall. Your toys we divided up, half in one house, half in another. It was a temporary shelter and we did not put down roots.

During our first weeks and months there we made an effort to be glad. The days passed. We found a kind of routine. You spent every other weekend with your father, the rest of your life with us. After school I took you by the hand and scrambled with you through the nettles, through the gap in the wire, and out on to the path. We walked the track between our house and the park until you were sure, quite sure, which hole in the hedge led back to your home.

Jim went on trying to reach you. Not with verbal intrusions the way I did but with small simple deeds of friendship. One Saturday he came back from the second-hand shop carrying a tall stool for you because you could not reach the table to eat comfortably on an ordinary chair. When he brought out his tools and began to take the thing apart piece by piece you allowed yourself a flicker of interest.

'What are you doing?' you asked, crouching down beside him for a moment.

'Chopping it up for firewood. It's no good, is it?' Jim teased, reading your thoughts.

You were not sure. You had not yet learnt to read his face, nor to tease him back.

'What *are* you doing?' you repeated, creeping nearer.

'I thought you wanted a stool.'

'Yes I did, but why are you taking it to pieces?'

'Small pieces burn better,' Jim said, straight-faced. He gave nothing more away so you wandered off in a sulk to play with your toys inside.

When you came back out the stool was intact, rubbed smooth with sandpaper and gleaming with new varnish.

'Why's it tied up with string?' you asked, staring in disbelief at the transformation.

'Don't you like the string? I thought it looked rather nice. A finishing touch.'

'Take no notice of him,' I interrupted, seeing another cloud of doubt cross your features. I wrapped my arms around you and hugged you close. 'The glue's still wet. The string's only holding it together until it sets. Doesn't it look lovely?'

'Come here,' Jim called.

You tolerated his arm around your shoulders while he showed you the stool.

'Look Tom, you can see the different woods. The seat is made of teak. That's why it's come up that deep reddish colour. Do you like it?'

'Yes,' you said.

You liked it, but you squirmed away from Jim's embrace. You did not like him.

The summer passed. September came, and one misty morning Jim took you fishing. I watched you skip along beside him, until you crossed the road and turned out of sight down an alley. You made your way between the houses and out into the open field of bumpy hummocks, brambles and cow parsley. The footpath was barely worn, as if no one bothered to make the short trip to the water, and you made fresh footprints in the wet springy grass.

A new concrete weir spanned the river. Over the top-solid rectangular stepping stones before the solid glistening sheet of water cascading over the edge. Half-way across, you stopped, clinging to each other, feeling in your bones the ice-cold rush of water.

After what seemed a long time, you moved on and settled to watch for sticklebacks on the last stepping stone before the bank. It was not quite as easy as you had imagined. You thought they would swim into your net but instead they darted, clusters of silver flickers in the water, anywhere, everywhere but near it. You flayed after the retreating fish with your arm outstretched. Maybe for a moment you felt disappointment. Then, keeping hold of a handful of your jumper in case you fell in, Jim showed you what to do.

'You see it's no good sticking in your net after they've passed,' he told you calmly. 'The trick is to position your net ready and wait for them to swim next to it.'

He made you wait patiently, quietly. Very still. The sticklebacks veered right then left towards your net, you flicked your wrist and pulled your net clear of the water. Twisting and thrashing in the green twine was your first fish. You closed your small hand around it and felt it squirm, slippery and lithe. You dropped the jiggling silver thing into the beer mug and gazed at it over the rim.

You came home radiant – two fish in a beer mug, pink patches on your white cheeks, and a face turned up in admiration to a man trying to be your father. It was the closest you two came to making it.

Dear Tom,

The months passed. You settled at school. Jim drove the motorway, a hundred miles each way, travelling to a university that was too far away. Sickened with doing nothing, with my own lack of purpose, I began to tap on my typewriter. In that grim backyard, in the vacuum that my life had become, I started to write. At first it was a way of filling time but later I was drawn to it and could not leave it alone. It became a necessity. A part of me.

One afternoon, I had dragged out the kitchen table searching for the autumn sun. There would be precious few days left when I could work outside. I broke off to collect you from school. I sat with you, my mind elsewhere, while you ate your biscuits and slowly sipped your juice, then I asked you to go and play. It was not usual, to leave you like this to your own devices, but that afternoon, the sun and the words flooded the paper and I had to continue. If I was not quick, they would fade. But you were there. You placed your hand on the table. You leant against me, willing me to stop.

'Why don't you go and explore? You know the

way to the park now. Go and play there for a bit if
you want.'

'I don't want to.' You kicked up the loose stones
around my chair.

'Why not? It's the only way you'll meet other
children. Go on, love. You've been hanging around ever
since you got home from school. I think you should go
and play on your own for a bit.'

'You come with me.'

You were determined to stop me. You stood your
ground, and the silent sentences scattered like seeds
in the wind.

'Please leave me alone to get on with this. Go on.
Go and play on your own. And please put away that
miserable face and find a cheerful one instead.'

'I haven't got a cheerful one,' you solemnly replied.

'Yes you have,' I said.

'I haven't. I've lost it.'

And so you dragged off down the path. Sinking your
shoes, left foot, right foot, in the deep earth at the
bottom of the garden, you started a slow, hard climb.
In slow motion you hoisted yourself up to the fencing
beyond, then hung for ages, dangling with barely a
movement from a branch of the yew tree. Finally,
with one quick last turn of the head in my direction,
you vanished through the hole in the hedge. But my
concentration was broken. I knew that a small child
scuffed his shoes along the dusty path and kicked up dirt
against the unfairness of it all. I knew that my small son
went nowhere after all but hovered beyond the fence and
waited for time to pass. I knew that he had one last look
for the face his mother wanted and could not find it.

Dear Tom,

Only the swing brought you peace and gave you back your day-dreams. Do you remember? From the distant path, you would scan the line to see which ones were occupied because it was important to swing in the red one, the last one in the row. If it was free, you raced ahead of me up the hill, leaving me panting behind. If a child already sat in it, you plodded up more slowly, then waited by the post, twizzling round and round on the shiny paint until you could run and seize it for yourself.

You asked to be pushed hard and high. Higher than any of the other mothers pushed their children. You yelled to be pushed until the chains jerked at the top of their arch above the supporting rail.

'Up you go! Up into the clouds!' I chanted for you.

You liked to be pushed for hours on end. Pushed into rhythmic oblivion. You sailed up into the sky and left your mess of a life behind. The whoosh of air cut off my voice, blocked my hopeless explanations. You hung your head back until your yellow mop of hair brushed the concrete, and the pieces of blue and white sky swam together.

Long after I stopped pushing you would stay in your seat.

'Not yet. Not yet,' you pleaded when I stirred and made signs that we should move on.

And on the way back downhill the good feelings evaporated and you scuffed your feet and tensed your small body, resisting me once again.

Back on the dusty path, you leant away from me and let go of my hand. Still too fragile, my happiness wavered. I had put on a brave face for you, but inside I too was full of sighs. Again and again you defeated me. You led me to despair. I felt the hopelessness of ever winning you round. I asked you why you would not try harder to like Jim. I asked you why you were being so awkward. I asked you why you would not make an effort, the slightest smallest effort, to be glad. And all the time I knew that I was chipping away at the good hard shell that the swinging had formed around you; poking at your bubble of calm because I was restless and tense and desperate. You heard my questions, just as you had heard them a hundred times before. In the long silences I left for you to fill, you concentrated on your small feet in their red and navy pumps, watched them kicking up the stones and the dust. You would say nothing.

Finally, back at the hole in the hedge, I turned you by the shoulders to face me and willed you to make contact with me.

'Answer me,' I ordered. 'Will you try harder?'

Your six-year-old will was immense. You lifted your eyes from the track and stared at me in blank and total refusal.

I found myself shouting, shaking you, 'Will you please talk to me! All you do is stare at me with those dead sheep's eyes. I've spent half my afternoon trying to cheer you up and it's got me absolutely nowhere!'

You stared steadily and directly through me. At the end of my tether I felt my arms reach out and give you a good hard shove.

'I give up!'

You sat in the dirt. I scrambled back through the hole in the hedge, as close to tears as you were.

From here, we went from bad to worse, a mother and son each damning the other's chances of peace and happiness. With your blank face and down-turned, silent mouth you could make me tremble with anger. Pitted against that silent withdrawal, I could feel myself losing control. Always, the louder my rage, the quieter your response. I wanted toys flung at my body and abuse at my soul and afterwards a hug to lift the clouds and clear the air. But you knew that. Clever Tom. You knew how to wind me up until my spring just broke.

One tedious, empty Friday you made the fatal mistake – pestering me once too often when I was preoccupied and anxious and worn out with your coldness.

You trailed behind me down the stairs as I struggled with a heavy pile of dirty washing, filling my time with mindless tasks because there was nothing else to do, unable to work because you would not leave me the space to be alone. I knew I was using energy which would otherwise have been channelled into temper or tears.

'Will you play with me?'

'Can't you see I'm busy! If you've got nothing better to do you'd better go and tidy your room. And don't make a song and dance about it. Get on with it and then I'll do something with you.'

This was the main arena for your passive confrontations, and there was nothing I could do about it. Over the years I had tried gold stars, threats, bribery, the lot. Nothing had the slightest impact. It was important for you to establish your right to live like that. Because it was one of the few things which annoyed me.

'Tidy your room *now*,' I said, calmly enough.

You wandered around, gazing at your Lego, picking up the odd brick or sock. Then you sat Buddha-like, and stared into space. I felt your stubborn resistance like a solid wall.

'Tidy up your mess,' I said more briskly. 'Come on. It won't take you long.'

Like a paraplegic snail you crawled to a small heap of junk and began to sift through it.

'Look, I'm not going to stand here all day,' I snapped. 'It's perfectly straightforward. Start with the books. Put them back on the shelf. Then the clothes into the dirty washing basket. Call me when you've got that far.'

When I returned half an hour later you were sitting in the same position but in a different spot, still staring at some point in distant time. You challenged me with your stillness, your inertia, your silence. Your face, a mask of sullen hostility. At your side, a wet flannel and greasy blue marks on the carpet.

'What are you doing? What are you doing with that flannel?'

'A bit of my face-paint got on the carpet. That's all. I was just wiping it up.'

'Not with a face-cloth you're not!' I retorted. 'Show me where it is.'

I took a second, harder look and realised how much greasy blue stuff you had smeared over the furniture, into your clothes, across the walls.

'*And* you've not picked anything up! Have you?'

You said nothing. You stared at me from across the

room and said nothing. And for the first but not the last time I said the one thing a child like you should not have to hear.

'I'm sick of you. Sick of your miserable face. Jim and I would be happy if it wasn't for you. You cause all our problems. Why don't you go and live with your father and leave us alone? That's what this is all about. That's what you really want.'

I stomped across the room, grinding crayon into the ugly rented carpet, breaking fragile Lego constructions, tearing paintings. You turned your passive, pale face to mine and I hit it. I hit my damp squib of a child, my frosty icicle of a little boy. My child who sat like a road-block in the way of my happiness. Three times, maybe four, I raised my hand and hit out against your impossible sullen resistance. Your eyes brimmed with tears but your body stayed limp. Your self-control was amazing. I hauled you off the floor and shook you. Tried to shake you into understanding what you were doing. To me. To us. To yourself. I tried to shake you alive, make you warm and responsive. Tried to light a flame in your numb and helpless soul.

I hit you and shook you and finally hurled you like a raggedy-doll right across the room. You lay against the wall, motionless. Even then, you did not respond. You said nothing, did nothing. My fury was spent and I thought you were dead.

Later, trembling, I wiped your face with tissues and stroked your damp hair. But I could not smooth away what I had done. For both of us, it was a watershed. I had gone past the point of no return and you would not forget or forgive. You would hold it against me. I would never forgive myself.

The next day you were more silent, watchful and wary. You recoiled from my touch, shied away from my pleading glances. Your body bore the marks of beating and I was appalled. I wept. I approached you with a new calm but the damage was done.

Dear Tom,

Some time after that, we moved north across the border to new jobs, new territory, a new start. You began a jet-setting life of super-shuttle trips between us and The Headband, hauling a rucksack and wearing headphones. Eventually, you took it all in your stride.

You grew used to the Victorian flat. Grew used to its tenement stairs, its shared back green, its view of the Pentland Hills. You grew used to a room we painted red for you and pasted with posters of wild cats before the Heavy Metal brigade usurped them. You grew used to the short route between the flat and your school. Grew used to a new small half-brother. Grew used to being part of a family which was finally whole. Even so, you made sure we never quite closed around you. You positioned yourself apart. To one side.

For a time, The Headband became Father Christmas, the Great God, the Perfect Parent. Because he saw you only on high days and holidays he showered you with attention and treats and presents. But your friends were here and as time went on, you made the trip south less often. Eventually you left him behind. The Headband became some cross between a distant relative and an old friend. He was no longer your father.

Part 3: Adolescence

Dear Tom,

You seemed to pass through puberty overnight. One day you were a little boy just starting secondary school and the next you were in the shower with a mass of dark pubic hair. You hid your nakedness from me behind doors and large towels. Your voice broke to a deep brown tone reminiscent of The Headband and you developed that hunched, loping, stylised walk copied from your Heavy Metal heroes. You disguised your slim shoulders and slight build beneath trailing layers of black T-shirts topped with mutilated denim. Your thin legs you shoved into miners' boots. You had lots of look-alike friends, and an organised philosophy of rebellion. Your peers and your idols preached a hard, silent breed of hostility. Your character crystallised and set. There was a malevolent screen of peer group pressure, a solid wall of group disapproval and I didn't know how to get over it.

The trooping past and vanishing acts into your bedroom began. Slowly you severed your room from the rest of the house, the rest of us. But my study with its glass door, *en route* to the no-go area of your sanctuary, afforded me a spy's eye view of the steady stream of pre-pubescents who stomped through the flat. At about third year they hit adolescence with a vengeance and size nine boots, awkward, gangling creatures who had not yet adjusted to their height or the breadth of their shoulders. From my vantage point I caught glimpses of tongues poking from oversized trainers, the jangling junk and paraphernalia of Heavy Metal, girls' legs in women's-land-army boots. The folk to whom they belonged vanished into the hell-hole. They avoided eye-contact. Ignored me, a mere adult, until I felt I did not belong in my own home. Do you remember, once in pique, I stuck a notice on my door saying 'La Concierge'. Good job none of them could remember much French.

For years I was the unofficial annexe of the school canteen. Here you could play your music and roar at the computer screen and ignore your mother in her kiosk trying to get on with her work. I would brace myself for the uproar as you and your friends hurled yourselves through the front door at twelve-fifteen.

I watched the stampede across communal ground to reach the protected space of your room. Saw the startled looks on the faces of your friends in the early days if I popped my head round your door and asked them if they would like a drink or something to eat. You'd think I had offered them a poisoned chalice not a cup of tea to warm their cold little souls. I soon learned to drop all that maternal hospitality crap. It was the last thing you wanted, a Posy Simmons mother with a nice smile and a plate of digestive biscuits. Looking as if she might actually want to take care of you.

Other mums told me that in the privacy of closed

rooms their tough teenage sons still had a soft spot for them. When the other thugs were not around, they could expect the odd kind word or a quick hug. They got the occasional good deed and caught a softness in their big kids' eyes. From you there was no warmth. No contact. There was nothing. Between us, the foundations were too shaky.

You said I was too strict. You said I did not give you the freedom you wanted. Didn't I know that all your friends were allowed out until the reasonable hour of one in the morning? Didn't I understand that their mothers trusted them to be sensible chaps who could find their own way home across the city long after the last bus had stopped running? Didn't I appreciate that you were singled out as the only teenager in the entire school who was asked to come home at some dumb specific hour? Well, that was our rule and we stuck to it. And you determined to undermine it.

It was the start of your relentless, tedious, escalating game of 'Beat the Clock'. No matter what time we asked you to be back by, you would be sure to miss it. Not now and again. Every bloody time. You would arrive home, perfectly, just ten or fifteen minutes outside the agreed deadline. And so it became a rule we couldn't relax, an arena for an epic battle.

'If you can't get your arse back here by eleven, you'd better be in by ten-thirty.'

'Christ, I was only ten minutes late last night. Come on. That's totally unreasonable. That's crazy.'

'Ten-thirty,' Jim repeated. 'And if you want to argue about it, it will be ten. Okay?'

So you came in at ten-thirty-five or ten-forty. And I lay in bed and fumed for half the night.

In the end you were grounded, and after many months of brinkmanship you had to concede temporary defeat. And then a change in tactics. A variation on the grudging theme. The phone would ring twenty minutes before you were due. Loud music in the background and you trying to sound reasonable.

'Hi Mum, can I have an extension?'

I would look at my watch – there was no way you could possibly make it back in time now, whether I said yes or no.

'Everyone else is staying until midnight and we're having a really good time. Oh, go on.'

'All right, just this once.'

But the phone calls went on, every single time you went out. They crept nearer and nearer to the time you were due back, and finally overtook it. Instead of lying awake waiting for you, we waited for the phone and the usual debilitating late-night confrontation.

In the end, as usual, you pushed us too far.

'Mum, it's me. Can I have an extension?'

'For Christ's sake, Tom, it's after midnight! You were supposed to be here half an hour ago! What's the point of ringing now? I was in bed trying to get some sleep!'

'Oh I just thought it would be okay. Everyone else has stayed on. Anyway I can't get home now until Simon's dad comes to collect us. I've missed the last bus.'

'Tell the bugger to walk home NOW!' Jim roared through the wall.

We lay awake discussing your behaviour until the

early hours, round and round the same old insoluble loops in the worn-out tape. You arrived home two hours late, surly, petulant, challenging, and were grounded again.

Dear Tom,

Then there was your room. Your womb. An endless source of antagonism. Well-meaning friends advised me to ignore it. It was his space. Let him have it. And in theory I agreed. But maybe they did not have in their houses a cesspit on the scale I did. And there were days, my 'ratbag' days as you and brother Iain termed them, those corkscrew tight forty-eight hours before the onset of a period when I developed an unnaturally fierce house-cleaning, nest-building urge. Everything had to be cleared, sorted, colour coded and smoothed out. On those days I couldn't stand your room. I wanted to hire a huge industrial vacuum cleaner and suck all the ancient stinking garbage down the tubes. Instead, I worried away at the edges, stooping to pick a crisp packet or crushed biscuit from the rubble, urging you to clear up, please, just once.

Then of course I blew. I walked in one day when you were at school and was rocked by the seething state of it. I had never seen anything so disgusting. I had spent night after night fretting and fuming at you, losing sleep. I had watched you in the morning, sullen and hostile, cruel and bitter. And now this. Something in me snapped. I kicked open your door so violently it slammed against the wall, chipping plaster on to the carpet. I hurled your possessions indiscriminately on to the floor, at the computer screen, even out of the window. You must have come home to utter devastation. But you never even mentioned it.

Jim on the other hand played the Room Game strictly by the book. He did not approve of my inconsistent behaviour nor my monthly amateur dramatics. Occasionally he passed comment. 'Look either make an issue of it and make the bugger keep his pigsty clean, or leave it alone. You can't have it both ways. You decide if you want to spend the amount of energy it will require to get him to live in a state which satisfies you.'

He contended, in that calm, logical way of his, that your room was not what was important. Other things were. 'His room is his affair. It doesn't matter. What matters is that he refuses to do anything for anybody.' All said in a nutshell. Jim expected some minimal form of help. Some sign of effort. Some give as well as take. Some small share in the boring communal chores. Others would shop and cook, clean and hoover, wash and iron, but you could do the few tasks we asked of you. Jim spelt them out. Over and over again. Feed the cats, clean out the fish, and empty the kitchen bin. Not heavy demands. Just a small contribution to help us out. To show willing. And, of course, you were not prepared to do it. Rather than comply, you provoked us with your relentless, predictable performance.

'Tom, you haven't emptied the bin.' First polite reminder.

'Tom.' Second reminder.

Third reminder.

Then the roar from Jim.

'Empty the fucking bin, Tom!'

And then, on one famous occasion, when Jim's nerves were more than averagely frayed – wham! He lifted the bin, marched grimly towards you, and tipped it over your head.

And there you sat – strands of spaghetti, drips of red sauce and bits of mushroom spread in your blond hair. You didn't even lift your head from your comic.

Despite the seeming crudity of method, I think Jim handled you better than I did. He was right. Why nag on about your room? It's your affair. Concentrate on basic house training. Empty the dishwasher. Empty the fucking bin. Tell us where you are. Come home on time. Ignore the house-rules and you get your head shoved in the garbage. Toe the little line we have drawn for you and somehow we will manage to jog along together.

But you did not like lines, did you, especially ones laid down by your parents. Not even little ones. Okay, then, it was battle lines if that was what you preferred. And sometimes you would find your room beaten up and your head crowned with pasta.

Can't you see, it was because you refused to express any kind of emotion. You cultivated a cool, nothing-to-get-heated-about stance to everything from the trivial to the catastrophic. Nothing penetrated your shell of shrugged-off apathy. Not shouting. Not slapping. I wondered what would touch you.

Jim was more phlegmatic than me. After the first years of trying, he ignored you most of the time. You two were like wallpaper to each other. Ships that passed in the night. Most of the time, you had a sort of amicable non-relationship. Left to your own devices, I wonder if you two might have pulled through. But I chewed away at the same old bone, trying to suck warmth and bonding out of my cold-growing child.

Dear Tom,

And then there was the bloody fish tank. All we asked from you was to occasionally clean the inside of the glass.

'Fish can't see out,' Jim would announce ominously at the dinner-table. Communication between you two was by now bare bones only. Jim had stopped wasting words. Head down, you would not reply.

'Did you hear?'

'Yeah.'

A few days on there would be another reminder. The following week, a third. I saw the signs and knew what was coming. Knew you would not comply until Jim had you pinioned against the wall.

'Why should I do it!' you would mutter between clenched teeth.

'I don't see why you shouldn't,' I would reply.

'Why doesn't he bloody do it if it bothers him that much?'

'They're your fish, not his.'

So you would dab at the glass with the scourer, casual, energyless, not even bothering to roll up your sleeves leaving smears and blobs, putting in the absolute minimal effort. Doing exactly what drove us insane.

And next time we all sat down to a meal, Jim would ask, 'Is that supposed to be clean?'

'Yeah.'

'Come here.'

You would scrape back your chair, swagger over to his side. Tossing back the blond locks. Defiant. Looking daggers.

'I said clean out the bloody tank, not dabble your fingers in the water!'

'I did clean it out . . .'

'Don't give me that crap. I said, clean it out! Got it? Understand?'

And, because you could not, would not, concede to wipe the insides of the panes of glass thoroughly now and again, you got landed with the lot. You had to spring-clean the entire tank so the fishes could see out again.

You dreaded it. I don't know why. Maybe because it required a bit of planning, some physical effort, and your presence for more than five minutes in our shared territory. Maybe just because it was an infringement of your liberty. Iain and I would exchange conspiratorial looks and run for shelter. You, cursing and swearing, swallowing defiant pride, would get out the green coils of hose-pipe, would ram one end on the tap. Close to weeping, with anger and frustration at being coerced against your will, you would collect the fish in the sieve, plonk them in the pressure-cooker. Up-end the massive tank on to the rolling-pin, stretch the hose to the tap. Sometimes I peeped in, knowing how much you despaired, trying to offer moral support if nothing else. There would be water spurting out all over the floor, trails of green hose-pipe across the kitchen. There would be gravel on the table and the sink full of smelly shells. And you, furious, fuming with the injustice. 'How am I expected to keep one hand on the fucking tap and one hand half-way across the fucking kitchen holding this end here in the tank!!'

Your face would be grimy with dirt and tears.

And you would leave the floor flooded, the fish water murky, stones unturned. As if to say, none of you can make me. None of this can force me against my will. Nothing you say or do will make me contribute willingly. Or well. I would cajole and persuade, but you would stomp off, stomp out of the flat, and I would cover up your failure, mop up the remains myself, frightened of further conflict.

But one day you were too laid back, too slow, and Jim walked in, tense and tired from work, and saw the half-hearted effort, the half-done task, the mess, the defiance in your eyes. He said nothing. There were no more warnings or reminders or one-more-chances. He simply took you by the scruff of the neck and dragged you over to the tank. On your face, a look of naked terror wiped out the sneer. He thrust your head and all its long streaming hair down into the tank. Your mermaid locks swam out like seaweed under water and the fish darted for cover.

'Better see for yourself. Have a look out from the inside. Have you done what you were asked? Is it clean? Is it!'

Like everything else we asked you to do, like every other small contribution we asked of you, it was more important to resist than to comply. You kept it up. Kept it up for years. Looking back, I see your childhood as a huge heavy stone we had to try and roll uphill.

Dear Tom,

Try to understand, it was what you did not do which defeated us. It was the way you fended us off. Kept us at arm's length. It was your indifference. Your cold detachment. You took no interest, no part, in anything we did or felt or cared about. In the end you were a boy hermetically sealed from the rest of the family, a growing child who took board and lodging, but wanted nothing, gave nothing in return. We were a family of three, committed to each other, involved with each other, plus one unconnected being, living his own steely, separate existence.

A robot could have done my job. Meals on wheels and a washing-machine would have served you just fine. I did not know what to do. You did not want me. You did not want any of us. You were a dead emotional weight occupying part of our space only because it was convenient.

I would come home to the thumping sound of your music. You and three or four others closed off in your room. Through the shut door I heard the loud matiness and *bonhomie* you gave your friends, and learnt to skate around your amputated existence. To take a wide berth in case I inadvertently knocked into you. If we collided, I held my breath and waited to be ignored. Or rubbed up the wrong way. Or made wretched by your looks of loathing.

'Oh . . . Hi, Tom . . .'

Hostile stare. Clicking of fingers to loud Heavy Metal. A shake of your long hair and a quick swivel on your heel and you were back in your room.

Some days, when I knew you and your mates were the flat, I delayed coming home. Rather than face the insolent looks on your faces, the studied ignoring of my awkward, tentative presence, I would hang around the shops or force my unwilling feet on an extra circuit of park and gardens. I did not want to go home. I did not want to tread on broken glass or stumble on hidden grenades. You made me feel superfluous and stupid and clumsy. I could not relax in my own home when you were there. I monitored your presence, your comings and goings, and heaved a sigh of relief when the front door closed behind you. Cold, critical, hard-hearted child, you oppressed me. The way you looked at me, and through me, and past me, you were de-skilling me as a mother.

But maternal hope sprang eternal, even then, and I was able to fool myself that deep down you cared. Coming home from a conference in Australia, jet lagged, shaky kneed, elated to have travelled so far on my own, I stood dazed on the doorstep. The tenement door was locked so I rang the bell. Surely you were home, because I had phoned from the airport to tell you to expect me. I rang again. Your face appeared in the bay window and disappeared again. I waved. I waited. I stood on the pavement in the howling wind and waited some more. I rang the bell again, long and loud and urgent, and at last you pressed the buzzer letting me into the stair. There I stood, in the dark, dank stairwell, with one enormous suitcase, one rucksack, and a carrier-bag of presents.

I wedged my foot in the front door, kept my finger on the bell, and when you buzzed back, I shouted into the intercom,

'The door's already open! I'm in. Aren't you coming down to help me!'

The thought of welcoming me had not crossed your mind. Your mother was back from the Antipodes with a ton of luggage and you had no plans to make it down the tenement stairs to help her. I had been back five minutes and my hackles were up, my heart pounding. You appeared on the stairs, casual, yawning, your bare feet stuck hastily into your untied boots.

'Oh, hello. Are you back?'

'You might have come down of your own accord! I do have a lot to carry.'

I was almost in tears. For me there had been time and space a million miles away to think it all through again, to resolve to try harder, to make a go of it with you. For you, nothing had changed.

'There's not that much.'

You grabbed the heaviest bag and stomped up the stairs, leaving me behind to struggle with the rest.

My suitcase you parked in the hall. You were lounging on the sofa, feet up. Not looking at me. Loud music pulsed from the speakers. On the floor, cassettes and my guitar and comics and dirty plates.

'Revising,' you announced, tongue in cheek. 'Fucking exams on Monday.'

'Would you turn down the music please. I've been

travelling for two days and two nights and my head hurts.'

Not rushing, you complied. You returned to lie across the chair, humming, head down. The silence was appalling. Worse than the throbbing music. Finally you looked up from your book and shook back your hair. Challenged me to say something.

'So, you've been working hard?'

'Not really. Just started today.'

'I've had a really good time.'

It was hopeless. The spontaneity had gone.

'Oh yeah. Good. Good.'

The leaden silence again. You yawning and stretching and scratching. Then you flung down your notes.

'Mat's broken off with Carol. Stupid bitch.'

'Oh. Has he?'

There was no more to say. You got up, jammed on your boots, and wandered off. Brushing past me, you left me standing, an unwanted stranger in my own house. A redundant mother.

Dear Tom,

Your next move proved the last little tap on our wobbly house of cards. It only needed a sigh, an exhaled breath, a fingertip touch of pressure. It tipped the balance and this family came tumbling down.

You turned down a month in California – a precious exchange with Jim's colleague in the States – so as not to be away from your friends. To my astonishment you said no thank you to four weeks off school, four weeks of cycling and skate-boarding around laid-back Stanford Campus, four weeks of bumming around in the sun. Testament indeed to the power of the peer group. You would have been in your element there.

You made your own arrangements. Fixed it to stay with Mat and his lenient, obliging mum.

I felt uneasy, but we needed this break, needed it desperately. And so off we went without you. Just the three of us. Secretly relieved.

And in that house of polished floors and many bath-rooms and oriental rugs, we slowly began to unwind. We lived each day, without anger or tension, amongst the lemon trees and humming-birds and camellias. I found out what it was like to walk calmly through the days, not wary of the hidden mines, not mindful of treading on broken glass, not rehearsing my words in case I said the wrong thing. Not waiting to bite my tongue or have my head bitten off.

But we had to go back. I returned, reluctantly, to the cold flat, and found utter chaos. In the kitchen, decaying food, mounds of unwashed plates and cups. In the bathroom, melting soap in a bowl of grimy water, black footprints in the bath. A filthy sink, sticky floors. The vacuum cleaner, my hairdrier, were broken. The larder was stripped bare and the cats were starving.

I asked you for an explanation.

'The place is filthy, Tom! I just don't understand it. Those people, living here, did they really leave it like this?'

You shrugged your shoulders.

'It's not that bad, is it? A bit untidy, that's all.'

'It's a bloody pigsty!' I exploded. 'It's going to take me hours to clean the place up.'

'Yeah, I came round a couple of times when they went off on trips to the Lake District. They were bloody untidy. I had to do their fucking washing up.'

I must have been very jet lagged to have fallen for that one, but fall for it I did. You sloped off and shut yourself in your room. You avoided me. Left me my boiling resentment. I felt violated, as if I had been robbed, my home infiltrated, soiled; my trust betrayed.

You heard us debate the state of affairs endlessly around the breakfast table. You saw me burst into tears as I cleared up the mess. You heard my indignation, my condemnation of these people. Finally, you watched me sit down and compose a letter accusing this woman of the patchwork quilts, pots of flowering violets and polished beechwood floors, of leaving my home a pigsty.

Ten days after arriving home I finally accused you of making the mess yourself. With a distraught letter from Stanford in my hand (another woman has been weeping, Tom), I accused you of lying to Mat's mother, of lying to me, but worst of all of allowing me to keep up the charade of believing you when all the evidence of my experience should have told me otherwise. I accused you of causing emotional mayhem in two otherwise rational families. I accused you of wasting a lot of people's valuable time. I accused you of breaking what little trust there was left between the two of us.

You admitted partial blame.

'Okay, so a few friends came round for the evening. We should have cleared up better. I mean, you're making a bit of a fuss, aren't you?'

Slowly the story unwound. You should have cleared up, yes, but that was only the tip of the iceberg. You should have told us the truth.

What actually happened was this. Our flat was empty for a week and you made the most of it. You and your mates set up alibis, twisted the Other Mother's bendy arm, jollied her into agreeing what a lark it would be to organise a jamboree in our absence, in our flat. Three girls set up a similar network of lies so that they too were available for a night. You and your buddies partied away in our flat until the wee small hours, then some of them went home.

You looked so amazed, my son, when I relayed to you the exact details of what actually happened the night before our return. (Gossipy neighbours should never be underestimated.) Three boys, three females, spent the night here. A letter, one of many you left carelessly in your jeans, for me to find in the washing basket, read: 'Dear Tom, Wild time last night!!! I hope Mat does not get Kate pregnant. Still I suppose that is their business.'

Tom, why did you lie? And carry on lying when you could guess what the consequences would be? Had you never heard of the camel's back?

Dear Tom,

Unable to face you, I retreated to my room, to my own private space. We avoided each other. We did not speak. Often in tears, I sat at my desk by the huge trailing ivy and stared at my screen. Days passed and I did nothing.

I could not concentrate. Then I tapped on the keys, and spilled into words some of the anger and some of the pain. I wrote for my own sanity. I wrote to try and sort through what had gone wrong, where I had failed. I started to write the story of your life. For hour after hour, day after day, week after week, the words flowed and the pain, slowly, began to ease.

But then, one morning, tense and tired, I started up my machine, and the writing I had worked on late into the night did not appear. I went hot and cold. Put my hand to my forehead, feeling the panic rise. Calm down, I told myself. This has happened before. Often. Until recently, the computer I did not understand had been our last grudging conversational link. If it went on strike, I was sunk. I would grind my teeth and fill my time with mindless jobs until you came home from school, then pounce on you before you were half through the door. Help me, I would cry, and you would brush me aside and work your quick-lightning fingers over the keyboard and make my vanished text reappear. You always rescued me, even if it was with sneering sarcasm.

There was nothing for it. Even in our sad state of siege, I would have to put our battle on the back-burner and jolly you into helping me. I knew it was pathetic of me. At that particular time, it was crass and selfish to break the silence between us to ask you to do anything. You were in your room. On study leave – ha! – because of exams. I tapped on your door, spoke tentatively to the star-burst of hair spread on the pillow.

'Tom could you help me please? I can't get the computer to work. I can't get on.'

You grunted.

'Please, Tom. I need help. I'm sorry to have to ask you. Please would you get up and sort it out for me.'

I waited an hour. Made myself a coffee. Put on a wash. Made the beds. Waited again. I knew you had come in very late last night. Then around midday there was movement and you stood, towering, glowering, at my open door. You were barefoot. You wore rags of jeans and an obscene T-shirt. You were days and days unshaven and your nails were black. Already the thud thud of Megadeth was pounding out of your room.

'I'm sorry to bother you. I know this isn't the best time . . .'

You shifted your weight to one foot. Watched with a half-smirk as I whined and wheedled. Watched me squirm, like an insect stuck by a pin.

'I've done all the usual things but the file is empty. You know how I panic. Oh God I hope I haven't lost it!'

You did not move.

'What are you looking for?'

It wasn't a question. More of a challenge.

'Oh, my own stuff. I told you about it. A sort of chronicle.'

'Yeah . . .' Your voice was heavy with sarcasm. You hammered your fist to the throb of Heavy Metal and bobbed your head like a chicken. Refused to meet my bewildered gaze.

Slowly, dimly, I began to realise.

'Look, Tom, it's the only way I can deal with all of this. To write it down . . .'

'It was a load of crap.'

'Pardon?'

'Crap. Libel. Rubbish.'

'What do you know about it? Who are you to judge?' My heart missed a beat. The look in your eyes set my cheeks burning.

'I read it. All of it. Last night. I tell you it's complete crap. It's your one-sided bloody version. It's lies, man. Fucking lies.'

'How dare you! How dare you read something that is private! No one, *no one* reads what I write. You knew it was something I was still working on. You had absolutely no right to read it.'

'I have every right. I'm entitled to know what you've been saying. It's me you're writing the lies about.'

After all that you had done, in our present precarious state, after all the trouble, all our anguish, still you were capable of this. For a moment I was too shocked to speak, and, taking advantage of my stunned silence, you swung round and stalked back to your room.

I scraped back my chair and made my shaking legs walk after you.

'So why can't I find it now?' My voice was trembling, barely audible against the hard howl of your Metallica.

'Because I wiped it off. It was so fucking disgusting I pressed the button on it.' You slammed your door and winched up your music a turn louder.

'You what? You did *what*?'

I was screaming like a fishwife. I was outside your room, banging my head against the door like one of your very own heroes. I felt devastated that you could have read something that was so private, destroyed something that was mine.

And of course I had not backed it up. I had

worked too late last night, and the previous nights, to think about saving it. You knew my standard of computer housekeeping. You would have known all that perfectly well. Forty or fifty pages were missing and I doubted if I could reconstruct them.

I was hysterical at the thought of my loss. I banged on your closed door with my fists.

'Come out of there! Turn that bloody noise off and get out here and help me see if it's still saved somewhere on the disc. For Christ's sake, Tom, help me find it!'

You sauntered out, glanced at me with steel-cold eyes, without a shred of sympathy. I gave you a shove towards my room, but you brushed off my hand as if it were a scorpion. You leant against the wall, chewing gum, yawning, looking at me as if I were filth.

'Find it yourself.'

'You know I can't.'

What an irony of a predicament. Me, blind bloody furious, but helpless. Mad, yet totally at your mercy. As you were perfectly aware.

'I'm not helping you find that crap.'

'You've no right to mess with my writing. How dare you!'

'How dare you write such shit about me?'

'Go and get it back!'

'Get it back yourself.'

Slam went your door. Up went the music again.

It was too much. You had stolen my writing. You had found my Achilles heel. You had found the way to retaliate. Sobbing, I ran to my study. I grabbed your framed photo which through all our fiascos had stuck it out stoically on my desk, and flung it at the wall, sending splinters of glass into the flowerpots, and the tissues and the papers fanned on my desk. Then I seized the paperweight. It was a heavy one, violets beneath blue glass. Perhaps you had stirred at the first sound of crashing glass. Perhaps you judged it wiser to emerge than let me run riot. When I hurled the paperweight at your door, you were already there, opening it. The missile caught you on the side of your neck. I saw you wince and put up your hand, but already I was shouting, 'Get out. Go away. I've had enough. Leave me alone!'

And you were shouting, 'Don't worry, I'm going. You don't think I'd fucking stay here with you!'

Dear Tom,

And so, my son, you left. Cleared out, decamped, took refuge with Mat and his bland mamma, your two staunchest allies. Your accomplices. I waited for an apology. Two apologies. I warned you that we did not want you home unless you could convince us that you would try to change. You waited for me to get things in perspective and to stem the flow of threats and accusations. Again, we were in stalemate.

After several weeks in our separate battle zones with no sign of a white flag, we asked you to come and talk to us. It was a ghastly situation. A formal invitation to one's son to return to his own home.

We sat like strangers in the lounge in a terrible silence which hung in the air like a thunder-cloud. I remember my hands were icy cold. I remember you sat slumped in the armchair with your long hair hiding your face. I remember the clicking of Jim's nails, the familiar give-away that he was churning inside out.

'Tom, do you have anything – *anything* – to say?'

'What is there to say?'

'Plenty, I would have thought.' Jim's mouth was pinched. I knew he was seething.

'I've said I'm sorry, but you're not interested in what I have to say and you don't believe me, so what's the point?'

'Do you realise what you have done?' I asked.

'I shouldn't have wiped off your writing. And I shouldn't have had a party while you were away but everyone has parties when their parents go away. I don't see why I'm being treated as if I've done something outrageous. They made some of the mess, anyway. You just want to blame me but it wasn't all my fault.' You were entrenched. You exuded disdain. You thought we were making a mountain out of a messy molehill. All your friends thought we had gone off the deep-end for nothing.

'I am sorry I lied to you. I've already said I'm sorry. But you go on and on. All I did was have a few friends round for the evening.' You swung your hair back from your dirty, unshaven face and glared briefly at us. As if we were the wrongdoers, not you.

'It's more to do with what you haven't done,' Jim said cryptically.

You were thinking of your mother's bad temper, of buddies and booze and dirty floors. We were talking about eleven years of civil disobedience. No wonder the conversation faltered. On you stumbled, doing your best to restate your position. Poor child, would you have fared any better if you had been armed with the honed debating skills of an articulate adult? In purely verbal terms, it was an unfair contest, an adolescent with a loathing of English faced with a tribunal of two adults who made their living by shaping words into coherent arguments. On that level, you did not stand a chance.

But in terms of stone-cold, stubborn entrenchment you were more than our match.

'If you weren't so strict with me I wouldn't have to tell lies,' you argued defiantly. 'I have less freedom than any of my friends. They're allowed out much later than I am. Their parents don't make them come in at eleven. You just treat me like a child. If you gave me more freedom I wouldn't have to find ways to get round the rules. You don't trust me. Mat's mother trusts Mat. She lets him do what he wants. She doesn't check up on him all the time and insist he comes in at some bloody stupid time on a Saturday night. They have an agreement that as long as he tells her afterwards, she forgives him if he's done something stupid.'

Well, that's lovely, isn't it? What a convenient arrangement. So Mat gets his girl pregnant and tells his mummy and that makes everything okay does it? Sorry. I expect more from you.

'You have to earn our trust,' was all I said.

But you battled on. Could you not *see* the look on our faces as you gave us not one inch? I felt your waves of antagonism slapping me in the face.

At last you got it out.

'You keep threatening to send me back to my dad. You've always done it. Ever since I was small. When you get mad, you go beserk and tell me I'm going to be sent away. And you won't believe me when I say it's not what I want. You think it is, but it isn't. I don't want to live with him.'

And with the pain came the tears, dripping down your nose and cheeks. But don't exaggerate, Tom. I said that to you about five or six times over a period of eleven troublesome, trying, testing years. I regret it. I threatened you because you drove me insane.

But this time it was not another threat. It was the only way Jim and I could survive outside a lunatic asylum.

Jim spoke, 'I've heard nothing from you to make me change my mind. If anything I'm more convinced that the decision we have come to is the right one. I'm a failure too. Maybe your father can do better.'

Your tiger cat jumped on your knee and you let your tears fall on him. For a long time none of us moved or spoke.

Dear Tom,

You must admit that we left you one last loophole. You could have wriggled out if you had really wanted, even though the threat of eviction was voiced and our final cards placed on the table. We offered you one last chance.

We made one more attempt to patch it up. We still hoped to put the past behind us and find a way for this family to exist together. We had booked a holiday in the Highlands, in a remote farmhouse set high on a cliff. You and your mate Simon, us and our friends. It was booked eons ago, it was too late to cancel, and the sea and the mountains and the islands just might put a different perspective on recent turbulent events. After arguments, tears, accusations, all of us could unwind in that wild place on the coast.

Jim, Iain and I drove up, trailing the dinghy, transporting bikes and boat gear pinioned to the roof-rack. Always on these long hauls up to the North West coast we felt the change of gear, we unwound as the landscape grew wild and rugged and mountain peaks towered, layer upon layer, against wind-swept skies. You and Simon travelled up by train because there was no more room in the car. Hilary and her son Luke would arrive later in the evening. So, the first excited entrance was ours. We knew the farmhouse from previous holidays, knew the steep, almost vertical climb up the rough track which led off from the road through the village. We could have revved up in the car, but if it rained the chances of getting back down through the ditches running with mud and loose stones were slight. We towed the boat to the marina below the farmhouse and left it ready for launching the next day. Then, like Sherpas, the three of us lugged our packs and boxes and domestic paraphernalia up the hill. We burst into the lovely old house, plain and shabby and gentle. I ran from window to window to gaze down at the misty islands and the glistening sea below. Jim brought up the bikes, set a fire blazing, wandered out on to the hillside. I made up beds, unpacked food, put a casserole in the oven, and music on the tape player. Iain checked out his old haunts – the games room in an outbuilding, the rope swing, the skid-run for suicidal bike runs. For a while it was possible to forget our family cold war.

Some hours later I spotted you and Simon pushing

heavy mountain bikes up the path. Two identical black skid-lids, two sets of ripped denim, two jaunty figures bearing massive backpacks climbing with the ferocious energy of youth. I opened the door and opened my arms to you. Over-enthusiastic, emotional from the beauty of the place, foolish, motherly, I said, 'Come in. Welcome. Isn't it wonderful? Let me show you round.'

It was a bit inappropriate, considering what you looked like, burdened, panting and sweating, after a four-hour train journey, a headlong ride to the village, and a haul up a vertical mountain slope. Simon, polite and cautious as the family guest, accepted it, however, in good faith. 'Yeh! Great!' he grinned as he dumped his pack on the doorstep.

You avoided my eyes, my arms. You brushed past me and spoke in the abrasive, angry voice I fondly hoped you might have left behind. 'We're perfectly capable of showing ourselves round.' You slammed your bedroom door on my clumsy attempts at kindness and another door closed inside me.

So, the tone was set. The fragile, hopeful atmosphere shattered. You exuded hate for the rest of the week.

You refused to get up in the mornings. You gauged my increasing irritation and developed a deliberate policy of rising later and later each day. You and Simon moved to mid-Atlantic time, rising about midday and staying up half the night. You joined our family outings, our hikes, our bike rides, our sails, only when it suited you. Simon, already implicated in our family's quarrels, took his cue from you. His early politeness faded into avoidance and finally rudeness.

Our friends stuck it out. Hilary witnessed my tears

and did her best to reassure me that your hatred was thin, that the antagonism would eventually fade. But she understood, as the days passed, that the wounds each of us had inflicted were too deep to be healed by the balm of one week's holiday. A sensible woman, she ignored your boorish manners and insolent behaviour. At dinner one evening, all of us seated around the huge kitchen table, hungry, wind-burnt and glowing after a long day's hike in brisk winds, Hilary brought a steaming rice-pudding from the oven and placed it before us.

'Looks like cat's vomit,' you kindly informed her. And snorted with laughter.

We took the homely upstairs bedrooms with the tiny casement windows, leaving you the incongruous pink room on the ground floor. Within twenty-four hours you created in this frilly boudoir a reeking, festering place of rotting food, empty lager cans and unwashed, wet clothing left in smelly heaps. When you were not risking life and limb on your bikes, this was where you squatted, listening to your Guns n' Roses, away from the open fireplace where the rest of us gathered each evening.

Remember the night of the World Cup semi-final – England against Germany? You boys in raucous mood, Jim jaunty, my outward jolliness admittedly only a thin veneer, but all of us game for a rowdy evening out. The only TV was in the snotty bar of an upmarket hotel on the shore. In we trailed in our waterproofs, obviously not their usual clientele. You, aggressive yet casual, slumped in a chair, with your boots stuck out, slovenly knocking back the pints Jim allowed you as a ritual accompaniment to a football match. Simon was more sober on a half pint of cider. Hilary's son Luke was curled up in unbearable anticipation inches away from the screen, biting his nails to the quick, barely able to watch. Iain sat straight, intoxicated by coke and the heady atmosphere, while we adults screamed like hooligans. The four Welsh yachties in identikit navy Guernseys who had dropped anchor to come ashore for the same event were frozen in excitement, forkfuls of scampi poised half-way to their mouths. The atmosphere was electric.

Even then, the last time we joined forces as a family, I watched you with dismay. Your long hair fell in greasy strands over your face. Your clothing looked as though it had been put through a shredder. You were adorned with lewd badges. But none of that upset me. It was the way you behaved as if I wasn't there. Or as if I were something nasty which had crawled out of the woodwork. Throughout the nerve-racking match the rest of us, children and adults, exchanged exultant glances of camaraderie as England battled on. We leaned on one another's shoulders, clapped each other on the back. We moaned with Gazza at the now notorious shedding of tears. Yet even in that hothouse atmosphere when social guards were dropped, you kept your back turned. You excluded me. You responded to my tentative smiles with venomous waves of hostility.

Maybe I should have wanted nothing. Yet for six long agonising days and nights I hoped for something other than a slap in the face. Perhaps I should have had it out with you then, told you what a disgusting rude bugger you were. I should have poured a bucket of cold water over the pair of you if you were not up by eleven in the morning. I should have said something.

Instead I let it fester. In the mornings, while you slept, I played Pavarotti louder and louder, in anger and despair and vengeance. I played it to wake you up. I played it to salvage my identity and my self-esteem which your adolescence was destroying. Preparing breakfast for the rest of the crew while you slept, I trembled with emotion, bottled up, not just from the endurance test of this so-called holiday but from years and years of battling with you. I wanted to slap you. Hit you. Shake you.

Why did you reject so uncompromisingly my last attempt to get close to you?

Towards the end of the week we said goodbye to our friends. We stood with hoods up against wind and torrential rain, while they packed themselves into their car. I burst into tears when Hilary hugged me. She knew what she was driving away from. We had talked. We had decided Jim and I needed the last two days to face you alone. Simon, therefore, was curtly driven to Oban to be put with his bike on the train home.

I had abandoned all pretence of motherly care. Instead of packing him a lunch for his journey, instead of taking the pair of you to the café with us for a last meal together, we dumped you both on the platform in the pouring rain, stuffed a couple of pound notes into your hands and told you to get yourselves some fish and chips. Jim's face was set. Rigid. But he kept a hand on my shoulder because he knew I might fall apart. When we found you, two hours later, and put Simon without ceremony on the train, you were both soaked to the skin, hair like black rats' tails dripping water down your faces. You looked cold and miserable. I could not care.

In the car, on the way back to the farmhouse, I sobbed my heart out because there was nowhere for us to go. We had come to a dead end. Iain was silent and alarmed. Jim drove, tight-lipped, furious that I was reduced to such a wreck. God only knows what you felt.

But I must not write this account as if the last violent emotions were mine. They were not. In fact it was you, not me, who cried the last tears.

That night, the night after everyone else had gone, we piled the hearth with pine logs and lit a crackling fire against the wind and rain outside. From the windows we could see the sky darkening and the masts of the boats bobbing like black sticks on the stormy water. I had done my crying and was calm. Jim sat in sombre mood by the fire, poking it to a brighter blaze, sipping his smoky-tasting whiskey. I think he had made up his mind that he could take no more from either of us.

I made the first move as you got up to stomp out of the room.

'Tom, please stay here with us. We need to talk to you. Whatever you have to say, I promise we will not shout. We won't swear at you. We passed that point long ago. We just want to hear what you have to say.'

Jim and I had already collaborated, agreed on the rules, decided, no matter what, to keep the tone calm. There were to be no outbursts that night. Just a terrible resignation and a knowledge, felt at least by two of the players in this final move in the game, that there was no turning back.

Perhaps you knew. Perhaps you didn't. You began to

weep. I don't know even then if you realised that you had overstepped the mark; gone beyond the point of no return. You knew something of what was coming but I suspect you thought it was to be yet another routine row.

I asked you, 'Why have you behaved like you have? Why so much hate?'

You tried to work out the state of play. Figure out our tactics.

'What do you mean?'

'You know what I mean. After all that we have been through, you came up here ready to hate and go on hating me. You have made no attempt to heal things.'

'Haven't hated you,' you muttered. You looked squeamish, sensing our contrived calm. You were trapped in an armchair again, forced to attend to another battering of adult argument. Screaming matches were easier.

'Just thought you were still angry with me and Simon about what we did while you were away. I thought you didn't want us here but you couldn't tell his mum it was all cancelled so we had to come. We just tried to keep out of your way because we knew you were cross. That's all.'

'Did my welcome look that way to you? Do you remember how I greeted the two of you?'

You would not meet my eyes. You stared at the carpet. You were writing your false scenario (did you admit this even to yourself?) but you needed your self-defence. You have always been quick with words.

But that last night of the holiday we knew that we couldn't go on. Jim said, 'Tom, I can't take any more.

I've had enough. Two weeks ago we told you that you would have to leave if you could not make some effort to change. I've seen no sign of a change of heart. No evidence whatsoever of a change of attitude.'

Difficult words from a philosopher to an adolescent. Hard words for the bravest of us to take in. But still you shut out the truth. You had stopped listening. You said nothing. I wonder if you thought it would all blow over, like a hundred hundred times before.

But the next morning we put you and your bike and your backpack on a train south. You were white with shock, and silent.

Part 4: Separation

Dear Tom,

You certainly cleared out, didn't you? Every trace. For a boy who never chucked anything away, however useless, however grotty, that's quite an achievement. The six red plastic washing-up bowls which served as drawers – empty! But I have grown used to them jammed shut with scrunched-up paper and every letter and postcard which ever fell on the doormat. Walls naked except for graffiti and blobs of Blu-Tack. Just the odd filthy sock left, six teaspoons, giant puff-balls of dust. And a year's supply of newspapers you were supposed to take for recycling. Barely a reminder that you lived here for seven years.

Dear Tom,

The last evening of our Highlands trip I had run in the floods of rain to the phone box in the village and dialled The Headband's number. I had told him his son would be on his way the next day. He had responded with condescending tolerance.

'Tom will be welcomed with calmness and kindness

at this end. I know something of what has been going on from his phone calls and I am certainly not prepared to heap blame on him as you have clearly done. It sounds to me as if he has taken enough.'

'Have you any idea what he has been like?' I shouted. 'I have tried to tell you what has been going on but you wouldn't listen.'

'Look, there are two sides to every story,' he had replied in hushed, dismissive tones. 'I am prepared to believe that Tom may have been a bit silly, that's all. He is only fifteen years old and he feels you have been very unreasonable.'

'Us, very unreasonable!'

'I'm prepared to offer Tom a home for the rest of the holidays while you two calm down and have a rest and get things back into perspective.'

Like you, The Headband thought it all a passing storm. It took another six weeks to convince him otherwise. Now, he is beside himself. He writes me indignant, righteous letters, pouring out volumes of bitterness, managing to cover pages with a fury which pushes his handwriting into crooked lines and forces his Biro almost through the paper. After ten pages or so I discover that my son is angry. Revelation! What did the man expect? Joyful gratitude?

But we remained adamant. You were to stay with him unless, and until, you could convince us in writing that you were willing to make some effort to change, to behave in a way which would allow this family to survive together again. Perhaps it was an unrealistic task for a fifteen year old but Jim had said, 'desperation can produce unexpected talent'. Perhaps we just expressed it badly, in language which was too adult.

You waited four weeks then wrote a short, polite letter, composed to a formula, nominally expressing the right kind of thing. An apology for the lies and the party. A promise that you would try harder. It would have got a Grade A at GCSE as an exercise in composition. But knowing you as well as I did, it didn't convince me. I read no hint of panic. No suggestion that you would compromise. If I had been marking your paper I would have commented: 'Could do better.'

What did I want from you? I wanted some sign of deep emotion. I wanted to hear panic on the end of the telephone. I wanted to read that you couldn't bear to lose us. What reached me, second-hand, via The Headband's laboured letters, was that actually you didn't like us very much, thought our handling of your adolesence outrageous, found our attitude to teenagers off the wall. But you were distraught about leaving your school and your friends. Sorry. I couldn't take that. And so for the time being you must stay where you are. You and The Headband would have to come up and collect your things.

You could have phoned and told me you loved me. But I don't think you do love me, so I congratulate you on a pride and honesty which prevented an easy lie.

Dear Tom,

School went back today. Your school, just across the field from the flat. For the first time in four years I must not expect a chance sighting of you from the kitchen window as you cross from one block to another. I must not watch for Mark's luminous green anorak, or Simon carrying his clarinet into the music rooms. But the habit dies hard. It's tough having a bird's-eye view of your child's school premises when your child is permanently absent. I feel that I no longer have the right to stare.

The phone attracts me like a magnet. I hover, in pathetic expectation. Yet the image of an ET-like Tom longing to phone home just doesn't ring true. You will brazen it out even if it breaks your heart. There is no reason beyond blind maternal optimism for me to believe that you would want to contact me. I ask myself what I would expect you to say and, I can't think of an answer. If I were in your shoes, I would not pick up the phone either.

Most nights I lie awake worrying about you. I suppose it's a case of better the devil you know for without any form of contact, my imagination runs riot. There are no images because no one tells me. I have no idea how you are coping. A relief, yes, not to have to bang my head against the brick wall of your antagonism, but alien and disconcerting to have an empty space where the brick wall used to be. I am amazed at how much I miss you.

Jim carries on. Unlike me, he can put the anguish of these days on the back-boiler and turn his mind to grant applications and departmental expenses and formal semantics. He does not say much about you. Just that he does not miss the tension. For him, I think, there is mainly relief. Like a large clockwork soldier, he briskly marches the route to and from the university, carrying his heavy old satchel. He values the new calm me and the gentler atmosphere in our home. We have no need to be alert, wary, cautious. We are beginning to unwind. Smiles are creeping back across our faces.

Iain is at school, knowing you will not be here when he comes back. I do not know what impact your leaving will have on him. I know that the strain of recent months had made him withdraw to his room, into himself. Wise beyond his years, he had become wary of causing the slightest extra ripple in our domestic waters. I am glad that a child of ten no longer has to wear a tin hat or step over sandbags in his own room.

He thought briefly about taking over your territory. Able to cover any amount of space with his layouts which grow like Topsy as he plots his intricate imaginative games, for a while he liked the idea of so much room on your platform. After school one day when he was feeling weary he tried having a nap up there, but the vibes were wrong and he rejected it in favour of his own familiar den. You know your brother. Although he toyed with the idea of decamping, he could not actually do it. Everything holds memories, associations, his past. Remember how he beat Jim with his fists at the age of five when we sold the old yellow Citroën. It was the only car he had known. Thrashing about like a wild thing, ready to run down the road after it, he had to be held down, screaming and kicking, while the buyer drove it away.

Iain is as different from you as chalk from cheese. Remember the baby monkeys? The ones offered the

choice of a hard wire mother which gave sustenance
through a bottle, or a soft cloth mother which gave
warmth and comfort but no food. Most of them chose
the second. Iain is a cloth monkey. You the other sort.
When he was young he clung to me with arms and legs
tightly wrapped round my body. He has fire in his belly
and passion in his soul. I understand this kind of child.
We understand each other.

To be honest, I didn't like the thought of Iain in your
space. At the moment I can avoid your room. If he had
moved in, I would have to face it each day. The red
room bears the lasting scars of your living; I prefer it to
stay that way.

Dear Tom,

Last night in bed, Jim and I were talking about you.
As usual, I was eager, trying to make sense of it all, he
was reluctant, knowing there is nothing more to be said.
Every night I turn off my bedside light at the end of
the same old tune. Who do you confide in? For weeks
after you left I would watch the whole of the news
before realising at the end that I had not taken in a
single word. I would lie in bed and turn pages of a
novel I did not read. Jim admitted that he too had a
monologue playing inside his head. Words and sentences
about you intruding into his work, his dialogue with his
computer, his conversations with colleagues. Images of
you overlaying his thoughts as he ran along his familiar
tracks. I thought it was just me but he said the record
played on and on in his head too. Strong, silent, stoic

man, I think he is suffering. Nowadays he just says that he tried for eleven years and failed. As if that were the whole story, beginning, middle and end. Perhaps for him it is. He says we achieve nothing by going over the same well-trodden ground. He also says it is a relief not to be the wall against which you are banging your head. I understand him. It is possible that he is beginning to let you go.

I ache to know what you are doing. How you feel. All connections are severed and I know nothing, apart from the few crumbs of information which The Headband drops me between the lines of anger. They don't satisfy a raging maternal hunger.

How are you?

What are you thinking?

Do you need me at all?

Dear Tom,

I am back in you room again and now I must tell you why. We are moving. At long last we have found an old stone cottage – a proper home – on the outskirts of the city. You won't have seen it, because, of course, you refused to join us on our endless house-hunting trips. You blocked your ears to talk of moving beyond the present convenient boundary walls of your school. But now it has all come together and we can go. What timing. Almost as if it couldn't happen until you were dispossessed. My mood is bitter-sweet. How can I celebrate, knowing your anger and pain? The joy of it must not bubble up yet, must be held at arm's length until I have faced the reality of the distance between you and me.

You will understand, I think. You remember a younger mum, don't you, who ran outside to scrape at the soil, to free a space for pale shoots, to tangle with overgrown climbers. It is twelve years since I had a garden of my own, but I had not reckoned with the likes of this one. It is more a place than a garden. There is a river and steep wooded banks and terraces and rockeries. There is a well where water drips through hanging curtains of ivy. It is miles away from the dust and dirt, the noisy squalidness and shoulder-rubbing of tenement dwelling. From the struggle and strife of the last seven years. You understand, don't you, my need for solitude? You know how I fretted in this flat, especially in summer with no front door leading to my own outside space. If I had to stay here for one more summer, I would be certifiable.

Every day now I stop the car after delivering Iain to his new school in the village. I get out and lean over the bridge which spans the river running through the new garden, and I feel the healing begin.

Dear Tom,

This letter should be marked *fragile* or *handle with care* because it is the last letter I will write you from your old home. What impact will it have on you?

It is very late. I am in our flat but it is no longer home. I am excited and wrung out with emotion like a child at Christmas. We got the keys to our cottage today. It was a brilliant, bright autumn day with leaves dropping like russet confetti from the vertical wooded banks into our ravine. The sense of belonging was immediate and strong.

When we go tomorrow will I leave you behind here? I asked a wise friend how I should say goodbye to you. She said, empty his room then place a candle where he spent most of his time. Light it so it will burn down on its own while you walk out for the last time.

I liked that idea. So I have cleared your room of all the things which crept back in after you left. I have put a candle on the shelf above the space where your computer used to be. Tomorrow evening, when the van is loaded, and Jim is waiting impatiently in the car, I will leave it to light up the space which was yours, and close the door on it.

Dear Tom,

That man is mad! Why on earth has he agreed to let you come back up here so soon after the trauma of leaving? Why send you on a school trip to Russia when it is no longer your school? When you have moved on.

I can't talk to him so I am writing to you. Telephone calls these days make me want to scream. I do scream. Twenty years in academia have rendered him incapable of normal conversation.

'I really cannot see any objections to his going. He feels strongly that he would like to travel with his friends and teachers. I feel it grossly unfair that he should have to miss such an opportunity. It is already arranged from this end. I have spoken to Mat's mother and she will organise his travel arrangements and offer him accommodation at either end of the trip.'

'But don't you see, it will set him back,' I exclaimed. 'You admit he has begun to settle down there. What's the point of opening up all the old wounds by rushing him back up to his old territory. I think it's a ridiculous idea.'

'So you want to deprive Tom of a chance of a lifetime's trip to Russia?'

'It is not a question of depriving him. It's a question of putting him in a situation for which he is not ready. It is too soon. He is still too raw.'

'I think I am in a position to judge that better than you. May I remind you that I am the one who has been dealing with him over the past three months since you threw him out.'

Long pause so I can register his righteous indignation.

'I did not throw him out. How many more bloody times do I have to tell you that life is not that cut and dried.' His instant summaries of our family's history provoke me every time, to respond when I should simply keep quiet.

'I think we have been over this particular argument before, and I wonder if there is much point in continuing, but as a matter of fact you did throw Tom out.'

'He threw himself out!' I shouted. 'You know perfectly well that he drove us mad with his refusal to take any part in our life. Never once did he do anything . . .'

'Let me take you back a stage in that argument, if I may,' he interrupted loudly.

'No, you may not. Go on. Go forward. Stop pretending this is a point-scoring exercise, or a public school debate, and let us try again to discuss our son and your insane plans to send him off to Russia!'

'Do you actually mean "never"? Do you actually mean that Tom never, literally never, not once in his life voluntarily helped either you or Jim . . .'

'Look, maybe he performed some minor act of kindness two or three times in his eleven years with us, but it is of no statistical significance! It does not matter. What we are talking about is his attitude . . .'

Another abrupt interruption.

'Could you give me a single concrete example of this attitude you keep referring to?'

I *am* screaming like a fishwife now, wanting to ram the phone down his stupid throat, 'Could you sum up in one concrete example why a relationship broke down? Could you?'

And so we go on. Hour after hour. He does not understand. He offers leaden phrases of intellectual argument and endless pained pauses which I jump in and fill with my quicksilver words. He tries to reduce eleven years of strife to one or two ordinary adolescent incidents. He wants to apportion blame. Then he might understand. The man has gelled in pedantry.

And he has the the final word on Russia. It seems that because I have handed you over, I have no say in the matter. Apparently you are arriving soon, back on your old stomping ground, to stay a couple of nights a few streets away, to take three weeks off your new

A level courses, to go on a school history trip to Russia when you have given up history and finished with the school.

Dear Tom,

Since The Headband would not tell us, we did not even know when to expect you. There we were, Jim and I, having a little stroll in the evening autumn sunshine, nudging each other at the 'For Sale' signs, grinning in relief because at last we could ignore them.

It was the funny orange frisbee I noticed first, the one like a mint with a hole we brought back from California, an obligatory present for Mat. It came flying across the road towards the gates, followed by loud hoots of laughter. I glanced up the road. Teenagers. A gaggle of them strung out up the road opposite. Then the shock of realisation. Not just any teenagers. THE teenagers. MY teenagers. I spotted Mat next, wearing a baseball cap back to front and prancing about in the middle of the fast-flowing traffic, leaping after the frisbee. Then Simon. Dreading what I would see next, I lifted my eyes to follow the line of youths to the straggling back of the group, to a couple with their arms entwined. No other than you, my son, with your left-behind girlfriend.

Mat actually managed a smile as he more or less ran us down. It must have been a left-over, middle-class reflex action. Others now were dancing across the road. You were clearly in view, smiling down at your girl, bending to kiss her.

For one long moment Jim and I were simply turned to

stone. For three months we had talked of you, thought of you, imagined you. Recently, not so urgently. I think, slowly, imperceptibly, we were letting go. Time was beginning to blur the sharpest images and to mute the harshest emotions. Then, without warning, on to this fading picture, a real you was superimposed. It was too cruel. My tears were instant, a primitive, maternal response to seeing you in the flesh. Jim tightened his grip on my hand until my rings cut into my flesh. Before you came any closer, before you reached the traffic island in the middle of the road, in the midst of a tide of rowdy youths who would have turned their loathing on us had they had time to register our presence, we blundered off in the opposite direction. We could not face you.

Dear Tom,

And then, the next day, you turned up again. But this time in the village – at our new house, in which I understood you were resolutely uninterested. The sun was pouring in through the upstairs windows. The sheep grazed quietly on the hills beyond. I was wandering happily, tape-measure in hand, when an oh-so-familiar voice wafted up the stairs. You actually managed to sound quite casual.

'Hi. Remember me?'

For a second I almost gave the game away. I felt the colour drain from my face. But I don't have a degree in drama for nothing. I gathered up my sagging jaw, held in check the ever-ready tears, composed myself as I moved across the landing.

You stomped steadily up towards me, and then, when we met at the top of the wooden stairs, your eyes, like mine, filled with tears. To my absolute surprise, you lifted your arms and hugged me. We stood there and held on to each other. Tom, you let your mask drop. Just for that one brief minute. I felt your need, as deep as mine.

But afterwards, you showed me only bitterness and savage anger. I expected no less. Jim appeared and exchanged brief neutral words with you. We offered you a lift back to town and, because it suited your arrangements, you accepted. You needed to be back at Mat's house that afternoon to pick up your things. The coach bound for Russia was leaving that evening. You told us between yawns that you had been up most of the night at a rock concert with a boy from the village. How on earth did you track him down in this remote outpost? You had not had a proper meal in twenty-four hours. You looked dirty, exhausted and wretched. Despite the spiked bracelets up to both elbows, despite what was left of the denim revealing shocking-pink boxer shorts, despite the multiple rings in your ears, despite the outrageous badges on your T-shirt – my son, you looked pathetic.

Is this The Headband's idea of giving you the freedom you craved? A ride through the city in the early hours of the morning in somebody's son's car? An empty stomach and a few hours' sleep on somebody's floor? Are you enjoying your new liberation? Or do you really want a warm bed, a bowl of home-made soup, and your mother's love?

Did you turn up out of spite? But, if so, why your

first reaction to me? And why have you buddied up, long distance, with the only boy in your former school who lives in this small village? Funny, I never heard his name mentioned among the many friends you talked about and brought home. Never saw his particular DM's treading across my carpet. How convenient for you, this sudden blossoming of a new friendship. Now you have left your mark and I am nervous. Could you not have left me this sanctuary?

Dear Tom,

That night, twenty minutes before the coach was due to leave the school gates for a trip half-way across the world, you turned up to ask for food for the journey. You had to swallow your pride and stand on our doorstep. Or you would have gone hungry.

I am quick in an emergency. In five minutes there was a Tom-worthy stack of peanut butter and strawberry jam sarnies, chocolate bars, apples and cartons of juice. You thanked me. You put a tentaive arm around my shoulders. Together we walked to the school gates. I looked neither to right nor to left at the other parents, unable to deal with their knowledge of what I had done, unable to cope with even one critical gaze. Boys were hugging girls. Girls were weepily hugging boys. Daughters were pecking fathers on the cheek. Sons were dissociating themselves from overfond mothers. The other kids looked smart – new anoraks and trainers, new holdalls. All in good warm clothing. All properly mothered and cared for. And there you were in a thin black Megadeth T-shirt and leaking canvas shoes. Did you not even have a coat to take to Russia? Tom, it's cold there, and you won't be able to buy a coat for love or money.

Mr McFarlane nodded his acknowledgement. Clipboard in hand, he shouted out the final orders and gave you the sign to board the coach. The atmosphere in the street was electric with emotion as you kids jostled to climb the steps.

You turned back. You came back to the spot where I stood alone and threw your arms around my neck before rushing headlong back into the crowd. It was a gesture not offered by any other child. Pretending to be just like the other ordinary mums, I waved and cheered until the back corner of the coach vanished round the corner. Pride alone kept my lips still and my face outwardly calm. But as the last goodbyes died away, and people walked slowly to their parked cars, I turned abruptly on my heel and hurried away before any one of them could hear the stifled sobs or see the tears which streamed down my face.

Dear Tom,

Oh surprise, surprise! The Headband reports that you have been unsettled for a number of weeks since your return from Edinburgh and your jaunt across the globe with your pals. Told him so! Well he can sort out the mess it has left you in.

Yesterday I imagined that here, in the quiet remoteness of this place, empty of old and painful memories,

I could almost forget about you. No, not forget. Just accept that you are somewhere else, someone else's problem.

But then you phone. After six silent months. I pick up the receiver and with a shock of recognition hear your voice, gruff, wary, hesitant.

'Hello.'

Bull's-eye! With one innocent word you shake me rigid. I try to calm a thumping heart and from somewhere find an unemotional, upbeat tone.

'Tom! What a surprise! How nice to hear your voice. How are you?'

You, voice dull and flat, 'Okay I suppose.'

I know you too well to let that pass.

'What does okay mean?' I ask as lightly as I can manage. 'How many on the Richter scale?'

'About two.'

'Out of how many?'

'About a hundred.'

You speak in a voice which is not jocular or cynical or taunting and I drop the bright, public persona.

'What's the matter, love?'

'Everything.'

Long distance I sense your sadness. There is no attempt at fake hilarity. I think I hear you stifling tears.

'What is it? Are you still missing your friends?'

See how transparent I am. We both knew what I really want to hear. I want you to say that it's me you're missing. That you need me. That you are unhappy down there. But you are too much in control to be tricked so easily.

'Not just that. The whole thing'

It was a long quiet talk. And although you did finally weep, you did not compromise. You couldn't, wouldn't give anything away. You somehow managed to convey the idea, without actually putting it on record, that you wanted to come home. But still you wanted it only on your own terms. Without our crazy constraints and confinements. Good, I thought. It is a start. At least you are shifting ground.

'Tom, if you want to come back we can talk about it.'

'I don't know.'

'Well, just remember, the option is still open.'

'It wouldn't work,' you replied. 'It would be exactly the same. Nothing has changed.'

You are right. Nothing has changed. Except that you have broken the long silence.

Dear Tom,

That night, after you phoned me, I had a nightmare about you. A horrible voiceless nightmare like a silent horror movie. It was a real video nasty, this one. We were back in the flat and you were taking a shower. I could see the outline of your body through the transparent screen. For some reason Jim sat on guard outside the bathroom, on patrol perhaps, or just lost in some absorbing paper about propositional logic. So it was left to me to watch your blurred hand reach up for the razor and slash across your wrists. The pale outline of your body was washed blood red. I tried to get to you. I tried to alert Jim. For God's sake, look behind you! Stop reading! Pay attention! But my voice and body were frozen and I had to watch you fold up into the bath.

Maybe I have been watching too much Hitchcock. I admit I am impressionable. I read recently that the actress in *Psycho* could not take a shower for twenty years after she made that film. But look at the transparent images in the dream. My terror that you might become despairing enough to kill yourself. The turned back of Jim. My inability to get through to you.

Sometimes I am seduced into an outrageous sequel to our domestic drama, a happy families scene in which you come home and all is forgiven. It requires a fair bit of self-deception, but I manage it. I imagine a new, nice Tom walking down the garden path in the glowing evening light. As if the real Tom were some kind of aberration. I bake your favourite chocolate cake and you sink into the sofa with the cat on your knee, oh so grateful to be back in the bosom of your family. You thinking, they are not so bad, after all, are they? It was just an awful mistake.

Then I pull myself up, sharp. There is no nice Tom, I remind myself, there is no nice relationship between us. But there is an honest Tom. You know, don't you, that all the tears in the world won't change the situation. You know that you can't come home. That there is no solution. That there is nothing either of us can do to knit up the enormous rift in the fabric of our lives. That we must live apart. It has taken me six months to catch up with you.

Dear Tom,

No. I can't accept the sad finality of that scenario. Your phone call gives me enough hope to think that, one day, you might, after all, come out waving the white flag. I gave it a lot of thought. I reasoned – he's down enough to pick up the phone, ring his mother after half a year's silence, and shed tears. Give him another few days and he'll be packed and waiting on the station ready to come home. It's just a matter of time. He's beginning to see it's not as green as it's grassy looking on the other side of the tracks. Maybe he's finally run foul of The Headband.

So I gave you a week. Then another week, resisting the daily temptation to pick up the phone. Let him simmer in his own bitter juices just a bit longer, I thought. Then I rang.

Okay, I give in. What happenened? What did I get wrong? No tears this time.

'Hi, Mum. Yeah, everything's fine. How are you? Cool! Cool! I mean chemistry's crap and one of my teacher's a fucking fascist, but yeah, it's okay.'

Hey, Tom, you're not even listening, and who is that female snickering in the background? Oh, sorry. You're a bit busy right now. Sorry I interrupted. You'll call me back sometime. Fine. Fine.

Next time, punch-drunk, I asked you outright. Before you hung up on me, I asked you why you sounded like a new person so soon after the avalanche.

'Tell me, what's happened since last time? I mean you were so upset, love.'

'Oh it just depends what's happened in the last twenty-four hours, I suppose. Not sure what you're on about.'

Cool Tom. Cold fish. You summed up your adolescent dealings with life so crudely. So well. At fifteen, is that all there is to it?

Okay, I am hearing you loud and clear. You are not at the station. Not on your way home after all. How dare you pull at my maternal heart-strings and then twang them back in my face? Hey, it hurts, you know.

Dear Tom,

Stop it, will you? Stop swinging from dull despondency to zippy *bonhomie*. You leave your mother staggering in the wake of your emotional roller-coasting.

Some nights it's the bright spark who lets little out of the emotional bag and accompanies his jocular, irreverent repartee with a twanging of chords played out for my benefit on a new and expensive electric guitar. I respond in kind. Jokes and jibes. Bitchy backchat and catty gossip. We are a good act. I can rise to the occasion, but afterwards there is a bitter taste in my mouth, because we have said nothing.

Other evenings over the telephone wires comes the sad, sullen Tom admitting to a shoulder-shrugging dissatisfaction with life down there. And in the next breath, knowing my eagerness, you add that it would be worse to be back up here. You talk for half an hour or more, holding me there at the end of the phone. Both of us cling on to our technological bonding.

We begin our practised verbal shadow boxing. You moving carefully around the ring with your muted dissatisfaction, your tales of woe. Me dancing after you with offers of reconciliation, of home-comings, but with strings still attached. You backing off. Me retreating. No, of course it wouldn't work. Silly to mention it again really. And through the gamesmanship your unspoken sadness.

'I'll be sixteen next week. I can leave home if I want. I mean (bitter laugh) you've already made me leave home, but you know what I mean (twang, twang). I can leave home properly (three chord sequence followed by a twiddly bit on the treble).'

'Where? Where do you propose going?'

'Anywhere. Under a hedge.'

And then I fall right down the trap you have set for me. I take you seriously.

'Isn't your old home, even with a few stupid house-rules, better than a hedge? We can negotiate.'

'Haven't got an old home!' you say quick as a flash. 'Haven't got a fucking home. Might as well go and live under a hedge.'

I panic.

'Surely we can work something out.'

I am down the pit and you chuck on the earth.

'Oh yeah!' you sneer.

So it's another sleepless night. Would he? Well, maybe he would, if only to spite me and the rest of the world. Or is it all a tease, a taunt to test your mother's nerves?

Another night. Another call. Oh sorry. No I didn't mean to take it all so seriously. Stupid of me to take you literally. Yes I do understand that you are really all right down there. Much better than up here with us. Yes, I will stop over-reacting. No, don't stop phoning. I need to talk to you. Please, keep the lines open.

Don't stop. Since there is nothing else I have to offer you, I can at least be an uncomplaining sponge to soak up your swings of mood. At least we are speaking to each other.

Epilogue

Dear Tom,

More than a year has passed. You phone me now and again to disturb the layers of emotional sediment which are gently settling now as seasons come and go, like seams of different-coloured sand. To some extent I have adjusted to our long-distance relationship. It is more manageable. Less violent. Easier on the nerves.

I wonder if this place has become a substitute for you. So much of my emotion is invested in it. I grow hardy in the cold air while I sweep up the leaves that fall as russet confetti into my wild unruly garden. The more in touch I become with the earth, the more out of touch I become with you.

I have been thumbing through this diary. If I am honest I must admit that this is what it has become. Perhaps these letters were never intended for the pillar-box. I accept that I have been writing as much for myself as for you. Here, living so peacefully, I am losing track of you.

I am aware that this is only my version of our relationship, our parting. What would your story have been if you had put pen to paper instead of me? Mine is biased, one-sided, incomplete. I have chosen some incidents, omitted others. Certainly they don't add up to the truth. But I have tried to sort things through.

I understand now that there is no single, simple explanation for what has happened between us. It has been a long, slow process like water wearing away rock. There are words, and there are images. Nothing is absolute. When you were small and I met you at the end of your day, I would bob down to greet you, but my open arms stayed empty. You would push me away, keep me at arm's length. Was there evidence even then of a hopeless incompatibility between a mother and her child?

Or, perhaps for you it was a simple question of betrayal. The replacement of one much-loved father for another who just would not do, no matter what he did or how hard he tried. I could blame Jim for what built up between us over the years with the weight of water behind a dam. The unwanted stepfather scenario would be a convenient peg on which to hang all the guilt. All the conflict. But then, as Jim rightly concludes, the real clash of wills was between you and me. I was the one who was incapable of relaxing while we occupied the same space. I was the one who tried to change you. Between you and him the bonding was not so highly charged, the attempts to reach you not so desperate, but then you are not his child.

Or, perhaps our conflict, like conflicts between other mothers, other sons, lies in a communal past. Our generation is as much to blame as yours. Through our own teens and twenties we marched to the sounds of our protests, determined to overthrow the harsh, set rules imposed on us. Now, as parents, we are disbanded. We are scared to impose barriers; frightened not to. There is no consensus. No unanimous backdrop of opinion. No agreement as to where we draw our lines. There has been a hard shift of power in your favour and we adults have lost our way. Some mothers hand over the keys, put in the ear-plugs, and hope that nothing dreadful happens. Others, with strait-jacket rules, force their kids into a double life of stifled manners round the dinner-table and a scandalous street-life outside. Through the most difficult years, as a mother I have felt unsupported, and very much alone.

For most mums, adolescence is just an awful phase to be endured. They know it will eventually pass. But from the time you pitted your three-year-old will against Maggie at the nursery, what was important to you was not to compromise. What mattered was your freedom to do what you wanted, to behave as you chose, irrespective of the needs and wishes of others. The way I see it most kids hit adolescence with a lot of emotional credit. They are building on years of a close, loving relationship. They owe their parents nothing. Parents owe their kids a lot. Joy. Laughter. Satisfaction. Slowly the credit diminishes as the kids get up to their teenage tricks but most get out the other side before they are bankrupt. But you entered adolescence already in heavy emotional debt. In terms of stubborn entrenchment, you have been an adolescent since you were three years old and have kept up your resistance like Chinese water torture ever since. I could not take any more.

Others mothers too have not survived. A friend of mine, driven to despair like I have been, hit her teenage son when she found he had been drinking himself legless and in return he pushed her down the stairs. She broke her arm. Later, when things had degenerated still further and she slapped his face for flinging abuse at her, he stuck the bread knife in her. How does a mother cope when her son grows big and stroppy? When you towered over me, Medusa locks, leather jacketed, Gestapo boots, four inches taller and three stone heavier, I lost the simplest way of admonishing you. A slap on the legs might have been better than all those years of bottled-up anger.

All this is rationalisation. Beneath it lies a deep well of emotion not so easily dredged up to the surface with words of explanation – my guilt and despair and sense of hopelessness as I watched myself losing you; your anger, your pain, your need to save face. Once we were just two, a pressured single mum and her recalcitrant child. There was stress and sadness, aching exhaustion, and no free and easy space when perhaps we could have sorted it through. I could not find the time, or the strength, or the right words to help you. I worried, and watched you. You withdrew. We lived in a hothouse of emotions. With our separate, urgent needs, we locked together in conflict, and dragged each other down. I imagine it like this – the two of us at the top of a snowy hill, climbing on to a sledge and setting off down the incline, clinging to each other. But the slippery slope becomes a vertical drop and soon we are hurtling down out of control. There is no getting off. There is no stopping. There is no scrambling back up to easy even ground. We have to go on until we hit rock bottom and are forcibly torn apart.

Once we had been set on that precipitous path, we could not help each other. Down we hurtled, no longer able to be ordinary or accepting or gentle with each other. We could not be just another mother and son. If only I could have grabbed your hands and looked at you and said, simply, please can we wipe it all out and start again. But in the end there was nothing I could do to placate you, except to totally sacrifice myself. Is that really what I should have done?

Last night I walked out into the night. The stars so clear. The air ice-cold. The fir, a forty foot sentinel beside the small stone cottage. Smoke from the chimney, a straight blue-grey line against the blackness of the sky. Sheep just visible, shapes, still as stones on the hillside. The sound of the river like the noise of the past running away downstream. I will stay here by the water. You will go your own way.

There is no more to say. These letters, or my journal, call it what you will – an attempt to make sense of why one person had to pack up their belongings and leave the person closest to him. In the end, Oscar Wilde said it all. He looked at the wallpaper in the room in which he lay dying, and said, 'I suppose one of us has to go.'

That's it really. In one short sentence.